FRENCH

...for better travel

2nd Edition

Travel better, enjoy more

ULYSSES

Travel Guides

Editorial *Series Director:* Daniel Desjardins; *Project Supervisor:* Pascale Couture.

Research and Composition Claude-Victor Langlois

Production *Design:* Patrick Farei (Atoll Direction); *Proofreading:* Jennifer McMorran; *Phonetic:* Pierre Corbeil; *Layout:* Isabelle Lalonde, André Duchesne.

Illustrations *Cover Photo:* Renzo Mancini (Image Bank); *Interior Illustrations:* Éditions Québec/ Amérique.

Offices
CANADA: Ulysses Travel Guides, 4176 Saint-Denis, Montréal, Québec, H2W 2M5, ☎ (514) 843-9447 or 1-877-542-7247, ⇒(514) 843-9448, info@ulysses.ca, www.ulyssesguides.com

EUROPE: Les Guides de Voyage Ulysse SARL, BP 159, 75523 Paris Cedex 11, France, ☎ 01 43 38 89 50, ⇒01 43 38 89 52, voyage@ulysse.ca, www.ulyssesguides.com

U.S.A.: Ulysses Travel Guides, 305 Madison Avenue, Suite 1166, New York, NY 10165, ☎ 1-877-542-7247, info@ulysses.ca, www.ulyssesguides.com

Distributors
CANADA: Ulysses Books & Maps, 4176 Saint-Denis, Montréal, Québec, H2W 2M5, ☎ (514) 843-9882, ext.2232, 800-748-9171, Fax: 514-843-9448, info@ulysses.ca, www.ulyssesguides.com

GREAT BRITAIN AND IRELAND: World Leisure Marketing, Unit 11, Newmarket Court, Newmarket Drive, Derby DE24 8NW, ☎ 1 332 57 37 37, Fax: 1 332 57 33 99, office@wlmsales.co.uk

SCANDINAVIA: Scanvik, Esplanaden 8B, 1263 Copenhagen K, DK, ☎ (45) 33.12.77.66, Fax: (45) 33.91.28.82

SPAIN: Altaïr, Balmes 69, E-08007 Barcelona, ☎ 454 29 66, Fax: 451 25 59, altair@globalcom.es

SWITZERLAND: OLF, P.O. Box 1061, CH-1701 Fribourg, ☎ (026) 467.51.11, Fax: (026) 467.54.66

U.S.A.: The Globe Pequot Press, 246 Goose Lane, Guilford, CT 06437 - 0480, ☎1-800-243-0495, Fax: 800-820-2329, sales@globe-pequot.com

Other countries contact Ulysses Books & Maps, 4176 Saint-Denis, Montréal, Québec, H2W 2M5, ☎ (514) 843-9882, ext.2232, ☎ 800-748-9171, Fax: 514-843-9448, info@ulysses.ca, www.ulyssesguides.com) **843-9448**

© January 2001, Ulysses Travel Publications
All rights reserved. Printed in Canada
ISBN 1894676009
Canadian Cataloguing in Press see p 5

SUMMARY

Cataloguing-in-Publication Data

French for better travel

2nd ed.

(Ulysses travel guides)

Includes index.

Text in English and French.

ISBN 1-89467-600-9

1. French language - Conversation and phrase book - English. I.

Series.

PC2121.F678 2000   448.3'421   C00-940748-9

FRENCH FOR BETTER TRAVEL

It goes without saying that French, like all languages, has its own share of nuances and subtleties, not to mention numerous regional variations. These will become more obvious to you as you go along and by paying special attention to locals, no matter what French-speaking land you find yourself in.

As several French sounds don't have any equivalent in English, we have strived to use a simple phonetic transcription system that allows for close enough approximations of French sounds. As such, we have rejected traditionally accepted methods (favoured by linguists but much too complex and "unnatural" for most people), as well as techniques popularized to the extent of meaninglessness.

In the end, we have retained an intuitive formula using familiar letter combinations and easily recognizable symbols where needed. Although these may often be juxtaposed in an unusual way, if you make the effort to produce the corresponding sounds by systematically following the rules presented herein, you will soon find yourself speaking the language of Molière without any embarrassment.

In order to keep things simple we have chosen not to elaborate too much on the variations that slightly modify the sound of several French consonants as compared to their English counterpart. Regular practice is the only way to notice and then reproduce them appropriately. The essentials of French pronunciation, as it differs from English, is thus explained in the basic rules below. Refer back to this section as you go and you shouldn't have any problem making yourself understood!

[a]	as in "bat."
[ay]	as in "say."
[e]	as in "bed."
[E]	as the "a" in "above." Be careful to always distinguish between [a], [e] and [E] when using the phonetic transliteration.
[g]	as in "glue."
[h]	Except when combined with "c" to produce the "sh" sound, this letter is silent in French.
[ng]	as in "ring."
[o]	Always pronounced as in "go."
[ø]	Always pronounced as in "got."
[œ]	Always pronounced as in "purse."
[R]	In French, the "r," either rolled or guttural, is always distinctly articulated. To remind you of this peculiarity, we have indicated it everywhere as "R." When audible at the end of a word, it

always seems to be followed, however faintly, by the sound of "E," as is the case with all other final consonants.

[s]   Always pronounced as in "**s**it."

[U]   This sound, which has no direct equivalent in English, somewhat resembles that of the "u" in "plural." We have put it in uppercase to remind you not to make it sound like a plain "oo."

[y]   This sound, which occurs quite frequently in French, corresponds to the "y" in "**y**es." When preceded by a vowel, it is generally underlined and separated from it by a dash to avoid any confusion with common letter combinations such as "ay" and "ey," which produce a completely different sound.

[zh]   This combination, which corresponds to the French "j," produces a sound resembling that of the "s" in "measure."

The following nasal sounds in French have no direct equivalent in English. Each of the letter combinations used to approximate them is to be treated as a single sound, and the final "ñ" is never to be heard as a distinct "n." Only by hearing them repeatedly from native speakers will you be able to recognize them and reproduce them properly.

[añ]	Pronounced as in "lawn" without articulating the "n."
[eñ]	Pronounced as in "length" without articulating the "gth."
[oñ]	Pronounced as in "tone."
[œñ]	Pronounced as in "open" without articulating the "n."

Other than the letter combinations [añ], [ay], [ee], [eñ], [oñ], [oo], [œñ], [sh], [zh] and [ng], which stand for a single sound, each and every one of the characters found between brackets must be distinctly heard.

GRAMMAR

Articles

Definite articles

Whereas there is only one definite article ("the") in English, there are three in French, to be used according to the gender and number of the names they are associated with: *le* (masculine - singular), *la* (feminine - singular), and *les* (masculine/feminine - plural).

le livre (the book)

la voiture (the car)

les voitures (the cars)

Note that *le* and *la* become *l'* in front of words starting with a vowel or a mute "h."

l'aéroport (the airport)

l'exposition (the exposition)

l'hiver (the winter)

Also note that *le* and *les* respectively become **au** and **aux** when they follow the preposition "*à*,"

Allons au (à le) festival (Let's go to the festival)

service aux (à les) tables (table service)

and become **du** and **des** when they follow the preposition "*de*."

le capitaine du (de le) bateau (the ship's captain)

l'horaire des (de les) trains (the train schedule)

Indefinite articles

Concurrently, there are three indefinite articles, also to be used according to the gender and number of the names they are associated with: **un** (masc.-sing.), **une** (fem.-sing.), and **des** (masc./fem.-plur.).

un éléphant (an elephant)
une étoile (a star)
des heures (hours)

Note that, unlike in English, the indefinite article is required in front of a plural noun.

Partitive articles

French also uses two partitive articles to distinguish the part from the whole, or things that cannot be counted: **du** (masculine - singular) and **de la** (feminine - singular).

du pain (some bread)
de la sauce (some sauce)

Gender

Unlike in English, French nouns are either masculine or feminine, but there are unfortunately no hard and fast rules, other than usage, to help you distinguish between the two except where they clearly depend on gender.

le père (the father)
la mère (the mother)

Nonetheless, you may find it useful to know that many feminine nouns naturally end in "*e*" or are formed by adding an "*e*" to their masculine counterpart (although corollary transformations are also sometimes required, such as doubling the final consonant or modifying the final vowel).

le voisin - la voisine (the male/female neighbour)
le chien - la chienne (the male/female dog)
le fermier - la fermière (the male/female farmer)

As for exceptions, they are numerous. For example:
the feminine of nouns ending in "***eau***" ends in "***elle***";

le jumeau - la jurnelle (the male/female twin)

the feminine of nouns ending in "***f***" ends in "***ve***";

le veuf - la veuve (the widower - the widow)

the feminine of most nouns ending in "***x***" ends in "***se***";

l'époux - l'épouse (the husband - the wife)

the feminine of nouns ending in *"teur"* ends either in *"teuse"* or *"trice"*;

le menteur - la menteuse (the male/female liar)
l'éditeur - l'éditrice (the male/female publisher)

the feminine of most other nouns ending in *"eur"* ends in *"euse"*;

le danseur - la danseuse (the male/female dancer)

and the feminine of many other nouns are completely different.

le garçon - la fille (the boy - the girl)
un homme - une femme (a man - a woman)
le frère - la sœur (the brother - the sister)

Plural

As a general rule, most nouns can be made plural simply by adding an "s" (sometimes an "x") to their singular form (pronunciation remains the same, however, the sole indicator of their number in spoken language is the article used in front of them).

un ami - des amis (a friend - friends)
un hôtel - des hôtels (a hotel - hotels)
un feu - des feux (a fire - fires)
un bateau - des bateaux (a boat - boats)

Notable exceptions are some words ending in "*al*" or "*ail*" whose plurals end in "*aux*" (which does change their pronunciation).

un cheval - des chevaux (a horse - horses)
un canal - des canaux (a channel - channels)
le corail - les coraux (the coral - the corals)
le bail - les baux (the lease - the leases)

Finally, certain words remain unchanged when pluralized,

une souris - des souris (a mouse - mice)
une croix - des croix (a cross - crosses)

while others follow unpredictable rules.

un œil - des yeux (an eye - eyes)
le ciel - les cieux (the sky - the skies)

Qualitative adjectives

In French, a qualitative adjective always takes the gender and number of the noun it describes (basically following the rules that apply to nouns), and usage, meaning or sound usually determine whether it goes before or after the noun.

un grand homme (a great man)
des hommes grands (tall men)
la belle fille (the beautiful girl)
les robes rouges (the red dresses)

Most qualitative adjectives can have three forms:
1) the generic, or **positive form**;

beau/belle (beautiful)

2) the **comparative form**, which serves to indicate varying degrees of a quality;

moins *beau/belle* *que* (less beautiful than)
aussi *beau/belle* *que* (as beautiful as)
plus *beau/belle* *que* (more beautiful than)

3) the **superlative form**, which serves to indicate the utmost degree (good or bad) of a quality,

> *le plus* beau / la plus belle (the most beautiful)
> *le moins* beau / la moins belle (the least beautiful)

or to emphasize the strength of a quality.

> *très* mauvais/mauvaise (very bad)
> *très* bon/bonne (very good)

Possessive adjectives

Whereas in English possessive adjectives appearing before nouns vary according to the gender and number of the "possessor(s)," in French they generally take the gender and number of the "possession," although their form also varies depending on whether there is one "possessor" or more.

	One "possessor"		
	One "possession"	Several "possessions"	
1st pers.	*mon* (m), *ma* (f)	*mes*	my
2nd pers.	*ton* (m), *ta* (f)	*tes*	your
3rd pers.	*son* (m), *sa* (f)	*ses*	his/her

17

mon portefeuille (my wallet)

ta valise (your suitcase)

ses chaussures (his/her shoes)

Two or more "possessors"

	One "possession"	Several "possessions"	
1st pers.	*notre* (m/f)	*nos*	our
2nd pers.	*votre* (m/f)	*vos*	your
3rd pers.	*leur* (m/f)	*leurs*	their

notre voiture (our car)

votre chambre (your room)

leurs billets d'avion (their plane tickets)

Demonstrative adjectives

The demonstrative adjectives, which also vary in gender and number with the nouns they introduce, are:

ce (masculine-singular), which becomes **cet** in front of a vowel or a silent "h";

ce chapeau (this/that hat)

cet homme (this/that man)

cette (feminine-singular);

cette auberge (this/that inn)

ces (masculine/feminine-plural);

    ces enfants (these/those children)

The Possessive Form

The possessive form is generally obtained by putting the object's complement in front of it, followed by *"de."*

    les plumes de l'oiseau (the bird's feathers)
    la robe de Stéphanie (Stephanie's dress)

Pronouns

Personal pronouns are further divided as:

Subject pronouns

I	*je*
you	*tu (vous)* *
he, she, it	*il* (m), *elle* (f)
we	*nous*
you	*vous*
they	*ils* (m), *elles* (f)

Object pronouns

me	*moi*
you	*toi (vous)* *
him, her, it	*lui* (m), *elle* (f)
us	*nous*
you	*vous*
them	*eux* (m), *elles* (f)

Reflexive pronouns (direct and indirect)

me/myself	*me*
you/yourself	*te, (vous)* *
him/himself, her/herself, it/itself	*le, lui* (m), *la* (f)
us/ourselves	*nous*
you/yourselves	*vous*
them/themselves	*eux* (m), *elles* (f)

* In French, *tu, toi* and *te* are only to be used when addressing a close friend, an intimate family member or a child. In all other dealings, it is to be replaced by *vous* (2nd person, plural), considered more polite and respectful.

Possessive pronouns, which take the gender and number of the "possession," have different forms depending on whether there is one "possessor" or more.

	One "possession"	Several "possessions"	
1st pers.	*le mien* (m)	*les miens* (m)	mine
	la mienne (f)	*les miennes* (f)	
2nd pers.	*le tien* (m)	*les tiens* (m)	yours
	la tienne (f)	*les tiennes* (f)	
3rd pers.	*le sien* (m)	*les siens* (m)	his/hers/its
	la sienne (f)	*les siennes* (f)	

Two or more "possessors"

	One "possession"	Several "possessions"	
1st pers.	*le / la nôtre* (m / f)	*les nôtres*	ours
2nd pers.	*le / la vôtre* (m / f)	*les vôtres*	yours
3rd pers.	*le / la leur* (m / a)	*les leurs*	theirs

GRAMMAR

Verbs

In French, the present tense of the indicative mode (as opposed to the conditional, the subjunctive or the imperative) only has a simple form, whereas the past and the future tenses each have simple as well as compound forms. Their various representations mostly derive from the infinitive, and some of them require the use of an auxiliary.

Infinitive verbs have four possible endings: **er**, **ir**, **oir** and **re**, and their present participles, or gerundives (which don't require the use of any auxiliary), all end in **ant**.

As for declined endings, they vary according to tense, person, radical and number, of which examples will be provided as we go along.

In the **present tense**, regular verb endings are generally as follows :

	Infinitive ending	**Present ending**
1st pers.-sing.	*-er*	*-e*
	-ir, -oir, -re	*-s*
2nd pers.-sing.	*All*	*-s*
3rd pers.-sing.	*-er*	*-e*
	-indre, -soudre	*-t*
	-dre	*-d*
	-ir, -oir, -re	*-t*
1st pers.-plur.	*All*	*-ons*
2nd pers.-plur.	*All*	*-ez*
3rd pers.-plur.	*All*	*-nt*

*je mang**e** (manger)* (I eat)

*tu prend**s** (prendre)* (you take)

*il/elle ser**t** (servir)* (he/she/it serves)

*nous aim**ons** (aimer)* (we like)

*vous voul**ez** (vouloir)* (you want)

*ils/elles dorm**ent** (dormir)* (they sleep)

The most usual simple form of the **past tense** is the **imperfect**, which indicates an habitual or ongoing action in the past.

	Infinitive ending	**Imperfect ending**
1st pers.-sing.	*All*	*-ais*
2nd pers.-sing.	*All*	*-ais*
3rd pers.-sing.	*All*	*-ait*
1st pers.-plur.	*All*	*-ions*
2nd pers.-plur.	*All*	*-iez*
3rd pers.-plur.	*All*	*-aient*

> *Je mangeais souvent une pomme le matin.* (I often ate an apple in the morning.)
>
> *C'est arrivé pendant que vous dormiez.* (It happened while you were sleeping.)

The most usual compound form is the **perfect tense**, which indicates an action completed in the past. It is obtained by using a declined auxiliary ("to have" or "to be") followed by the past participle of the action verb (which varies depending on the infinitive ending but remains unchanged through all persons).

	Auxiliary	**Past participle ending**
1st pers.-sing.	*j'ai / je suis*	*-é, -i, -is, -u, -t*
2nd pers.-sing.	*tu as/es*	*-é, -i, -is, -u, -t*
3rd pers.-sing.	*il/elle a/est*	*-é, -i, -is, -u, -t*
1st pers.-plur.	*nous avons/sommes*	*-é, -i, -is, -u, -t*
2nd pers.-plur.	*vous avez/êtes*	*-é, -i, -is, -u, -t*
3rd pers.-plur.	*ils ont/sont*	*-é, -i, -is, -u, -t*

GRAMMAR

*Je **suis** allé à l'aéroport.* (I went to the airport.)

*Tu **as** pris l'avion.* (You took the plane.)

*Elle **a** déjà su.* (She once knew.)

*Nous **avons** fini par arriver.* (We finally arrived.)

*Vous **avez** fait une erreur.* (You made a mistake.)

*Ils **ont** beaucoup voyagé.* (They travelled a lot.)

As for the **future tense**, verb endings are as follows and are generally tacked onto the verb:

	Infinitive ending	Future ending
1st pers.-sing.	*All*	*-rai*
2nd pers.-sing.	*All*	*-ras*
3rd pers.-sing.	*All*	*-ra*
1st pers.-plur.	*All*	*-rons*
2nd pers.-plur.	*All*	*-rez*
3rd pers.-plur.	*All*	*-ront*

*je mange**rai** (manger)* (I will eat)

*tu prend**ras** (prendre)* (you will take)

*il/elle servi**ra** (servir)* (he/she/it will serve)

*nous aime**rons** (aimer)* (we will like)

*vous voud**rez** (vouloir)* (you will want)

*ils/elles dormi**ront** (dormir)* (they will sleep)

The auxiliaries

The two main French auxiliaries are avoir (to have) and être (to be), of which *"avoir"* is the most common. They can be used alone or in conjunction with other verbs to form various compound tenses.

Avoir (to have)

Positive form		Negative form	
j'ai	(I have)	*je n'ai pas*	(I don't have / I haven't)
tu as	(you have)	*tu n'as pas*	(you don't have / you haven't)
il/elle a	(he/she/it has)	*il/elle n'a pas*	(he/she/it doesn't have / hasn't)
nous avons	(we have)	*nous n'avons pas*	(we don't have / we haven't)
vous avez	(you have)	*vous n'avez pas*	(you don't have / you haven't)
ils/elles ont	(they have)	*ils/elles n'ont pas*	(they don't have / they haven't)

*je n'**ai** pas mang**é*** (I have not eaten)

*tu n'**avais** pas pris* (you had not taken)

*il/elle **aura** servi* (he/she/it would have served)

*nous **avons** aimé* (we liked)

*vous **aurez** voulu* (you would have wanted)

*ils/elles n'**avaient** pas dormi* (they had not slept)

Être (to be)

Positive form		Negative form	
je suis	(I am)	*je ne suis pas*	(I am not / I'm not)
tu es	(you are)	*tu n'es pas*	(you are not / you aren't)
il/elle est	(he/she /it is)	*il/elle n'est pas*	(he/she/it isn't / isn't)
nous sommes	(we are)	*nous ne sommes pas*	(we are not / we aren't)
vous êtes	(you are)	*vous n'êtes pas*	(you are not / you aren't)
ils/elles sont	(they are)	*ils/elles ne sont pas*	(they are not / they aren't)

je suis *part*i (I left)

*tu n'é*tais *pas allé* (you had not gone)

il ne sera *pas ven*u (he would not have come)

The Negative Form

The negative form is generally obtained by putting "ne" ("n'" before a vowel or a silent "h") in front of the verb and "pas" after it.

Je ne veux pas y aller. (I don't want to go there.)

Ça ne fonctionne pas. (It doesn't work.)

Nous n'oublierons pas. (We will not forget.)

In the case of compound tenses, *"pas"* goes after the auxiliary but before the past participle.

> *Tu n'a pas mangé.* (You didn't eat.)
> *Vous ne serez pas partis.* (You won't be gone.)
> *Ils n'avaient pas dormi.* (They had not slept.)

The Progressive Form

In French, this form does not require any special construction, and although it can sometimes be rendered as *"être en train de,"* which translates as "being in the midst of" followed by an infinitive, it is most often expressed by a simple declined verb in the present, past or future tense.

Thus, to the question: "What are you doing?," someone may either reply: *"Je suis en train de regarder la télévision."* or simply *"Je regarde la télévision."* (I'm in the midst of watching TV). "What were you doing?" - *"Je regardais la télévision."* (I was watching TV).

The Passive Form

Just like in English, the passive form is obtained by using the declined auxiliary "*être*" (to be) followed by the past participle of the action verb.

Je **suis** bien **ser**vi. (I am well served.)
La **voiture** *é*tait **conduite par un** homme. (The car was driven by a man.)
Vous **sere**z **partis avant** midi. (You'll be gone before noon.)

The Interrogative Form

The interrogative form is usually obtained by simply inverting the verb and the subject pronoun.

Voule*z*-**vous d**anser? (Do you want to dance?)

When the subject is a noun, it goes in front of the verb all the same, but a corresponding pronoun must be added immediately after the verb.

Le **car** es**t-***il* **plein**? (Is the bus full?)

In the case of compound tenses, the subject pronoun goes after the auxiliary but before the past participle.

Avez-vous fait une réservation? (Did you make a reservation?)

And if the subject is a noun, the previously mentioned rule is to be similarly applied.

La température a-t-elle été clémente? (Has the weather been mild?)

(Also note that, in such constructions, a *"t"* always has to be added between two otherwise adjoining vowels.)

Irregular Verbs

Here are a few of the most common irregular verbs:

aller (to go)
  je vais (I go)
  tu vas (you go)
  il/elle va (he/she/it goes)
  ils/elles vont (they go)

j'irai (I will go)

tu iras (you will go)

il/elle ira (he/she/it will go)

nous irons (we will go)

vous irez (you will go)

ils/elles iront (they will go)

partir (to leave)

je pars (I leave)

tu pars (you leave)

il/elle part (he/she/it leaves)

nous partons (we leave)

vous partez (you leave)

ils/elles partent (they leave)

venir (to come)

je viens (I come)

tu viens (you come)

il/elle vient (he/she/it comes)

ils/elles viennent (they come)

je viendrai (I will come)

tu viendras (you will come)

il/elle viendra (he/she/it will come)

nous viendrons (we will come)

vous viendrez (you will come)

ils/elles viendront (they will come)

pouvoir (to be able to)

> *je peux* (I can)
>
> *tu peux* (you can)
>
> *il/elle peut* (he/she/it can)
>
> *nous pouvons* (we can)
>
> *vous pouvez* (you can)
>
> *ils/elles peuvent* (they can)

> *je pourrai* (I will be able to)
>
> *je pourrais* (I could)

vouloir (to want)

> *je veux* (I want)
>
> *tu veux* (you want)
>
> *il/elle veut* (he/she/it wants)
>
> *nous voulons* (we want)
>
> *vous voulez* (you want)
>
> *ils/elles veulent* (they want)

> *je voudrai* (I will want)
>
> *je voudrais* (I would like to have)

Yes	*Oui*	[wee]
No	*Non*	[noñ]
Maybe	*Peut-être*	[pœtetR]
Excuse me	*Excusez-moi*	[exkUzay mwa]
Hello	*Bonjour*	[boñjooR]
Good evening	*Bonsoir*	[boñswaR]
Good night	*Bonne nuit*	[bøn nUee]
Hi	*Salut*	[salU]
Goodbye	*Au revoir*	[o REvwaR]
Thank you	*Merci*	[meRsee]
Thank you very much	*Merci beaucoup*	[meRsee bokoo]
Please	*S'il vous plaît*	[seel voo ple]
You're welcome	*Je vous en prie (il n'y a pas de quoi, de rien)*	[zhE voo zañ pRee (eel nya pa dE dkwa, dE Rieñ)]
here	*ici*	[eesee]
there	*là*	[la]
left	*à gauche*	[a gosh]
right	*à droite*	[a dRwat]
straight ahead	*tout droit*	[too dRwa]

with	*avec*	[avek]
without	*sans*	[sañ]
a lot	*beaucoup*	[bokoo]
a little	*peu*	[pœ]
often	*souvent*	[soovañ]
sometimes	*de temps à autre*	[dE tañ za otR]
when	*quand*	[kañ]
very	*très*	[tRe]
also	*aussi*	[osee]
above (on, over)	*dessus (sur, au-dessus de)*	[dEsU (sUR, o dEsU dE)]
below (under, beneath)	*dessous (sous, en-dessous de)*	[dEsoo (soo, añ dEsoo dE)]
above	*en haut*	[añ o]
below	*en bas*	[añ ba]

How are you?
Comment allez-vous?
[kømañ talay voo?]

Fine, and you?
Très bien, et vous?
[tRe byeñ, ay voo?]

Fine, thank you
Très bien, merci
[tRe byeñ, meRsee]

Where is the...?
Où se trouve...?
[oo sE tRoov...?]

Where is the hotel... / the... hotel?
Où se trouve l'hôtel...?
[oo sE tRoov lotel...?]

Is it far from here?
Est-ce loin d'ici?
[es lweñ deesee?]

Is it close to here?
Est-ce près d'ici?
[es pRe deesee?]

Excuse me, I do not understand
Excusez-moi, je ne comprends pas
[exkUzay mwa, zhE nE koñpRañ pa]

Could you speak more slowly, please?
Pouvez-vous parler plus lentement, s'il vous plaît?
[poovay voo paRlay plU lañtmañ, seel voo ple?]

Could you repeat that, please?
Pouvez-vous répéter, s'il vous plaît?
[poovay voo Raypaytay, seel voo ple?]

Do you speak French?
Parlez-vous français?
[paRlay voo fRañse?]

I do not speak English
Je ne parle pas l'anglais
[zhE nE paRl pa lañgle]

I do not speak Spanish
Je ne parle pas l'espagnol
[zhE nE paRl pa lespagñøl]

Is there someone here who speaks French?
Y a-t-il quelqu'un ici qui parle français?
[ya teel kelkœñ eesee kee paRl fRañse?]

Is there someone here who speaks English?
Y a-t-il quelqu'un ici qui parle anglais?
[ya teel kelkœñ eesee kee paRl añgle?]

Could you write that out for me?
Est-ce que vous pouvez me l'écrire?
[es kE voo poovay mE laykReeR?]

What does that mean?
Qu'est-ce que cela veut dire?
[kes kE sla vœ deeR?]

What does the word... mean?
Que veut dire le mot...?
[kE vœ deeR lE mo...?]

I understand
Je comprends
[zhE koñpRañ]

I do not understand
Je ne comprends pas
[zhE nE koñpRañ pa]

Do you understand?
Vous comprenez?
[voo koñpREnay?]

In French, we say...
En français, on dit...
[añ fRañse, oñ dee...]

In English, we say...
En anglais, on dit...
[añ añgle, oñ dee...]

Could you show me in this book?
Pouvez-vous me l'indiquer dans le livre?
[poovay voo mE leñdeekay dañ lE leevR?]

Is there a...?
Est-ce qu'il y a...?
[es keel ya...?]

Could I have...?
Puis-je avoir...?
[pUeezh avwaR...?]

I would like to have...
Je voudrais avoir...
[zhE voodRe avwaR...]

I do not know
Je ne sais pas
[zhE nE se pa]

NUMBERS - *LES NOMBRES*

one	*un*	[œñ]
two	*deux*	[dœ]
three	*trois*	[tRwa]
four	*quatre*	[katR]

five	*cinq*	[señk]
six	*six*	[sees]
seven	*sept*	[set]
eight	*huit*	[Ueet]
nine	*neuf*	[nœf]
ten	*dix*	[dees]
eleven	*onze*	[oñz]
twelve	*douze*	[dooz]
thirteen	*treize*	[tRez]
fourteen	*quatorze*	[katøRz]
fifteen	*quinze*	[keñz]
sixteen	*seize*	[sez]
seventeen	*dix-sept*	[deeset]
eighteen	*dix-huit*	[deezUeet]
nineteen	*dix-neuf*	[deeznœf]
twenty	*vingt*	[veñ]
twenty-one	*vingt et un*	[veñ tay œñ]
twenty-two	*vingt-deux*	[veñt dœ]
thirty	*trente*	[tRañt]
forty	*quarante*	[kaRañt]
fifty	*cinquante*	[señkañt]
sixty	*soixante*	[swasañt]
seventy	*soixante-dix*	[swasañt dees]
eighty	*quatre-vingt*	[katRE veñ]
ninety	*quatre-vingt-dix*	[katRE veñ dees]
one hundred	*cent*	[sañ]
two hundred	*deux cents*	[dœ sañ]

38

five hundred	*cinq cents*	[señk sañ]
one thousand	*mille*	[meel]
ten thousand	*dix mille*	[dee meel]
one million	*un million*	[œñ meelyoñ]
two hundred fifty-two	*deux cent cinquante-deux*	[dœ sañ señkañt dœ]

TIME - *L'HEURE ET LE TEMPS*

when?	*quand?*	[kañ]
right away	*tout de suite*	[too dsUeet]
now	*maintenant*	[meñtnañ]
next	*ensuite*	[añsUeet]
later	*plus tard*	[plU taR]
often	*souvent*	[soovañ]
sometimes	*de temps à autre*	[dE tañ za otR]
Monday	*lundi*	[lœñdee]
Tuesday	*mardi*	[maRdee]
Wednesday	*mercredi*	[meRkREdee]
Thursday	*jeudi*	[zhœdee]
Friday	*vendredi*	[vañdREdee]
Saturday	*samedi*	[samdee]
Sunday	*dimanche*	[deemañsh]

day	*jour*	[zhooR]
night	*nuit*	[nUee]
morning	*matin*	[mateñ]
afternoon	*après-midi*	[apRe meedee]
evening	*soir*	[swaR]
today	*aujourd'hui*	[ozhooRdUee]
this morning	*ce matin*	[sE mateñ]
this afternoon	*cet après-midi*	[set apRe meedee]
this evening	*ce soir*	[sE swaR]
tomorrow	*demain*	[dEmeñ]
tomorrow morning	*demain matin*	[dEmeñ mateñ]
tomorrow afternoon	*demain après-midi*	[dEmeñ apRe meedee]
tomorrow night	*demain soir*	[dEmeñ swaR]
the day after tomorrow	*après-demain*	[apRe dEmeñ]
yesterday	*hier*	[yeR]
the day before yesterday	*avant-hier*	[avañ tyeR]
week	*semaine*	[sEmen]
next week	*la semaine prochaine*	[la sEmen pRoshen]
last week	*la semaine dernière*	[la sEmen deRnyeR]
next Monday	*lundi prochain*	[lœñdee pRosheñ]

January	*janvier*	[zhañvyay]
February	*février*	[fayvReeay]
March	*mars*	[maRs]
April	*avril*	[avReel]
May	*mai*	[may]
June	*juin*	[zhUœñ]
July	*juillet*	[zhUee-ye]
August	*août*	[oo]
September	*septembre*	[septañbR]
October	*octobre*	[øktøbR]
November	*novembre*	[nøvañbR]
December	*décembre*	[daysañbR]
June 1st	*le 1er juin*	[lE pREmyay zhUœñ]
June 10th	*le 10 juin*	[lE dees zhUœñ]
June 17th	*le 17 juin*	[lE deeset zhUœñ]
June 31st	*le 31 juillet*	[lE tRañtay œñ zhUee-ye]
month	*mois*	[mwa]
next month	*le mois prochain*	[lE mwa pRosheñ]
last month	*le mois dernier*	[lE mwa deRnyay]
year	*année*	[anay]
next year	*l'année prochaine (l'an prochain)*	[lanay pRoshen (lañ pRosheñ)]
last year	*l'année passée (l'an dernier)*	[lanay pasay (lañ deRnyay)]

41

What time is it?
Quelle heure est-il?
[kel œR eteel?]

It is	one o'clock
Il est	*une heure*
[eel e]	[Un œR]

two o'clock
deux heures
[dœ zœR]

three thirty / half past three
trois heures et demie
[tRwa zœR ay dEmee]

four fifteen / a quarter after four
quatre heures et quart
[katR œR ay kaR]

four forty-five / a quarter to five
cinq heures moins le quart
[señk œR mweñ IE kaR]

five after six
six heures et cinq
[see zœR ay señk]

ten to seven
sept heures moins dix
[set œR mweñ dees]

In fifteen minutes / in a quarter of an hour
Dans un quart d'heure
[dañ zœñ kaR dœR]

In thirty minutes / in a half an hour
Dans une demi-heure
[dañ zUn dEmeeyœR]

In an hour
Dans une heure
[dañ zUn œR]

In a minute
Dans un instant
[dañ zœñ eñstañ]

One moment please
Un instant, s'il vous plaît
[œñ neñstañ, seel voo ple]

I will come back in an hour.
Je reviendrai dans une heure
[zhE REvyeñdRay dañ zUn œR]

43

When can we have breakfast?

À partir de quelle heure peut-on prendre le petit déjeuner?

[a paRteeR dE kel œR pœtoñ pRañdR IE pEtee dayzhEnay?]

When can we have breakfast?

And until what time?

Et jusqu'à quelle heure?

[ay zhUska kel œR?]

When will the room be ready?

À quelle heure la chambre sera-t-elle prête?

[a kel œR la shañbR sERa tel pRet?]

When do we have to leave the room?

À quelle heure doit-on quitter la chambre?

[a kel œR dwa toñ keetay la shañbR?]

What is the time difference between... and... ?

Quel est le décalage horaire entre... et... ?

[kel e IE daykalazh øReR añtRE... ay... ?]

COUNTRIES AND NATIONALITIES
PAYS ET NATIONALITÉS

Argentina	*Argentine*	[aRzhañteen]
Australia	*Australie*	[østRalee]
Austria	*Autriche*	[otReesh]

Belgium	*Belgique*	[belzheek]
Belize	*Belize*	[bayleez]
Bolivia	*Bolivie*	[bøleevee]
Brasil	*Brésil*	[bRayzeel]
Canada	*Canada*	[kanada]
Chile	*Chili*	[sheelee]
Colombia	*Colombie*	[køloñbee]
Costa Rica	*Costa Rica*	[køsta Reeka]
Ecuador	*Équateur*	[aykwatER]
El Salvador	*El Salvador*	[el salvadøR]
France	*France*	[fRañs]
Germany	*Allemagne*	[almang]
Great Britain	*Grande-Bretagne*	[gRañd bREtang]
Guatemala	*Guatemala*	[gwataymala]
Honduras	*Honduras*	[oñdURas]
Ireland	*Irlande*	[eeRlañd]
Italy	*Italie*	[eetalee]
Mexico	*Mexique*	[mekseek]
Netherlands	*Pays-Bas*	[pay-ee ba]
New Zealand	*Nouvelle-Zélande*	[noovel zaylañd]
Nicaragua	*Nicaragua*	[neekaRagwa]
Panama	*Panamá*	[panama]
Paraguay	*Paraguay*	[paRagway]
Peru	*Pérou*	[payRoo]
Spain	*Espagne*	[espang]
Switzerland	*Suisse*	[sUees]

United States	*États-Unis*	[ayta zUnee]
Uruguay	*Uruguay*	[URUgway]
Venezuela	*Venezuela*	[vaynayzUayla]
I am...	*Je suis...*	[zhE sUee]
American	*Américain(e)*	[amayReekeñ(n)]
Argentinean	*Argentin(e)*	[aRzhañteñ(een)]
Australian	*Australien(ne)*	[østRalyeñ(n)]
Austrian	*Autrichien(ne)*	[otReeshyeñ(n)]
Belgian	*Belge*	[belzh]
Belizean	*Bélizien(ne)*	[bayleezyeñ(n)]
Bolivian	*Bolivien(ne)*	[bøleevyeñ(n)]
Brazilian	*Brésilien(ne)*	[bRayzeelyeñ(n)]
British	*Britannique*	[bReetaneek]
Canadian	*Canadien(ne)*	[kanadyeñ(n)]
Chilean	*Chilien(ne)*	[sheelyeñ(n)]
Colombian	*Colombien(ne)*	[køloñbyeñ(n)]
Costa Rican	*Costaricain(ne)*	[køstaReesyeñ(n)]
Dutch	*Néerlandais(e)*	[nay-eRlañde(z)]
Ecuadoran	*Équatorien(ne)*	[aykwatøRyeñ(n)]
French	*Français(e)*	[fRañse(z)]
German	*Allemand(e)*	[almañ(d)]
Guatemalan	*Quatémalthèque*	[gwataymaltek]
Honduran	*Hondurien(ne)*	[oñdURyeñ(n)]
Irish	*Irlandais(e)*	[eeRlañde(z)]
Italian	*Italien(ne)*	[eetalyeñ(n)]

Mexican	*Mexicain(e)*	[mekseekeñ(n)]
Nicaraguan	*Nicaraguayen(ne)*	[neekaRagwayeñ]
New Zealander	*Néo-Zélandais(e)*	[nay-ozaylañde(z)]
Panamanian	*Panaméen(ne)*	[panamay-eñ(n)]
Paraguayan	*Paraguayen(ne)*	[paRagwayeñ(n)]
Peruvian	*Péruvien(ne)*	[payRUvyeñ(n)]
Salvadoran	*Salvadorien(ne)*	[salvadøRyeñ(n)]
Spanish	*Espagnol(e)*	[espangøl]
Swiss	*Suisse*	[sUees]
Uruguayan	*Uruguayen(ne)*	[URUgwayeñ(n)]
Venezuelan	*Vénézuélien(ne)*	[vaynayzUaylyeñ]

ENTRANCE FORMALITIES
FORMALITÉS D'ENTRÉE

passport	*passeport*	[paspøR]
visa	*visa*	[veeza]
tourist card	*carte de tourisme*	[kaRtE dE tooReesm]
immigration	*immigration*	[eemeegRasyoñ]
customs	*douane*	[dwan]
luggage	*bagages*	[bagazh]
suitcase	*valise*	[valeez]
bag	*sac*	[sak]

the embassy	*l'ambassade*	[lañbasad]
the consulate	*le consulat*	[IE koñsUla]
citizen	*citoyen*	[seetwa-yeñ]

Your passport, please
Votre passeport, s'il vous plaît
[vøtRE paspøR, seel voo ple]

How long will you be staying in the country? (see p 39)
Combien de temps allez-vous séjourner au pays?
[koñbyeñ dE tañ alay voo sayzhooRnay o pay-ee?]

Three days	*Trois jours*	[tRwa zhooR]
One week	*Une semaine*	[Un sEmen]
One month	*Un mois*	[œñ mwa]

Do you have a return ticket?
Avez-vous un billet de retour?
[avay voo œñ bee-ye dE REtooR?]

What is your address while in the country?
Quelle sera votre adresse au pays?
[kel sERa vøtR adRes o pay-ee?]

Are you travelling with children?
Voyagez-vous avec des enfants?
[vwayazhay voo avek de zañfañ?]

gant[m]

skieur[m] alpin
alpine skier

handle
poignée[f]

wrist strap
dragonne[f]

ski pole
bâton[m] de ski[m]

ski stop
frein[m]

ski boot
chaussure[f] de ski[m]

basket
rondelle[f]

ski
ski[m]

heel piece of the binding
talonnière[f] de la fixation[f]

edge
carre[f]

ski[m] alpin
alpine skiing

ski hat
bonnet[m] / tuque[f]

ski glove
de ski[m]

ski goggles
lunettes[f] de ski[m]

ski suit
combinaison[f] de ski[m]

tip
pointe[f]

shovel
spatule[f]

toe piece of the binding
butée[f] de la fixation[f]

bottom
semelle[f]

Illustration by Québec/Amérique International © 1992

Here is the mother's (father's) permission
Voici le consentement de sa mère (de son père)
[vwasee lE koñsañtmañ dE sa meR (dE soñ peR)]

I am in transit
Je ne suis qu'en transit
[zhE nE sUee kañ tRañzeet]

I am on a business trip
Je suis en voyage d'affaires
[zhE sUee zañ vwayazh dafeR]

I am just visiting
Je suis en voyage de tourisme
[zhE sUee zañ vwayazh dE tooReesm]

Could you open your bag, please?
Pouvez-vous ouvrir votre sac, s'il vous plaît?
[poovay voo oovReeR vøtRE sak, seel voo ple?]

I have nothing to declare
Je n'ai rien à déclarer
[zhE nay Ryeñ a dayklaRay]

(air)plane	*avion*	[avyoñ]
boat	*bateau*	[bato]
train	*train*	[tReñ]
bus	*autobus*	[otobUs]
taxi	*taxi*	[taksee]
car	*voiture*	[vwatUR]
rental car	*voiture de location*	[vwatUR dE løkasyoñ]

I have lost a suitcase
J'ai perdu une valise
[zhay peRdU Un valeez]

I have lost my luggage
J'ai perdu mes bagages
[zhay peRdU me bagazh]

I arrived on flight number... from...
Je suis arrivé sur le vol... de...
[zhE sUee zaReevay sUR lE vøl... dE...]

I have not got my luggage yet
Je n'ai pas encore eu mes bagages
[zhE nay pa zañkøR U me bagazh]

Is there a bus to downtown?
Y a-t-il un bus qui se rend au centre-ville?
[ya teel œñ bUs kee sE rañ o sañtRE-veel?]

Where do I catch it?
Où le prend-on?
[oo lE pRañ toñ?]

What is the price for a ticket?
Quel est le prix du billet?
[kel e lE pRee dU bee-ye?]

Does this bus go to...?
Est-ce que ce bus va à...?
[es kE sE bUs va a...?]

How long does it take to get...
Combien de temps faut-il pour se rendre...
[koñbyeñ dE tañ foteel pooR sE rañdR...]

   to the airport?
   à l'aéroport?
   [a la-ayRopøR?]

   to downtown?
   au centre-ville?
   [o sañtRE-veel?]

By bus?
En bus?
[añ bUs?]

In a taxi?
En taxi?
[añ taksee?]

In a car?
En voiture?
[añ vwatUR?]

How much should I pay?
Combien faut-il payer?
[koñbyeñ foteel pe-yay?]

Where do I get a taxi?
Où prend-on le taxi?
[oo pRañ toñ IE taksee?]

How much is the trip to...?
Combien coûte le trajet pour...?
[koñbyeñ koot IE tRazhe pooR...?]

Where can I rent a car?
Où peut-on louer une voiture?
[oo pœtoñ looay Un vwatUR?]

Tourist office / bureau
Office de tourisme
[øfees dE tooReesm]

Tourist information
Renseignements touristiques
[Rañsengmañ tooReesteek]

Is it possible to reserve a hotel room from the airport?
Est-ce qu'on peut réserver une chambre d'hôtel de l'aéroport?
[es koñ pœ RayzeRvay Un shañbR dotel dE la-ayRopøR?]

Is there a hotel at the airport?
Y a-t-il un hôtel à l'aéroport?
[ya teel œñ notel a la-ayRopøR?]

Where can I change money?
Où peut-on changer de l'argent?
[oo pœtoñ shañzhay dE laRzhañ?]

Where are the... offices?
Où sont les bureaux de...?
[oo soñ le bURo dE... ?]

Public Transportation
Les transports en commun

bus	*bus*	[bUs]
tour bus	*car*	[kaR]
subway	*métro*	[maytRo]
train	*train*	[tReñ]
ticket	*billet*	[bee-ye]
return ticket	*aller-retour*	[alay-REtooR]
air conditioned	*air conditionné*	[eR koñdeesyønay]
video	*vidéo*	[veeday-o]
numbered seats	*place numérotée*	[plas nUmayRøtay]
reserved seats	*siège réservé*	[syezh RayzeRvay]
restaurant car	*wagon-restaurant*	[vagoñ RestoRañ]
train station	*gare ferroviaire*	[gaR feRøvyeR]
bus station	*gare routière*	[gaR RootyeR]
platform	*quai*	[kay]

Where can I buy tickets?
Où peut-on acheter des billets?
[oo pœtoñ ashtay de bee-ye?]

How much is it for...?
Quel est le tarif pour...?
[kel e IE taReef pooR...?]

What is the schedule for...?
Quel est l'horaire pour...?
[kel e løReR pooR...?]

Is there a fare for children?
Y a-t-il un tarif pour enfant?
[ya teel œñ taReef pooR añfañ?]

What time does the train leave for...?
À quelle heure part le train pour...?
[a kel œR paR IE tReñ pooR...?]

What time does the bus arrive from...?
À quelle heure arrive le bus de...?
[a kel œR aReev IE bUs dE...?]

Is coffee served on board?
Est-ce que le café est servi à bord?
[es kE IE kafay e seRvee a bøR?]

Is a snack served on board?
Un repas léger est-il servi à bord?
[œñ REpa layzhay eteel seRvee a bøR?]

Is a meal included in the price of the ticket?
Le repas est-il compris dans le prix du billet?
[lE REpa eteel koñpRee dañ lE pRee dU bee-ye?]

Which platform for the... train?
De quel quai part le train pour...?
[dE kel kay paR lE tReñ pooR...?]

Where do I put my luggage?
Où met-on les bagages?
[oo metoñ le bagazh?]

Excuse me, you are in my seat
Excusez-moi, vous occupez ma place
[exkUzay mwa, voo zøkUpay ma plas]

Which train station are we at?
À quelle gare sommes-nous?
[a kel gaR søm noo?]

Does this train stop in...?
Est-ce que le train s'arrête à...?
[es kE lE tReñ saRet a...?]

What is the closest station?
Quelle est la station la plus proche?
[kel e la stasyoñ la plU pRøsh?]

How much is a ticket?
Combien coûte un trajet?
[koñbyeñ koot œñ tRazhe?]

Is there a booklet of tickets?
Y a-t-il des carnets de billets?
[ya teel de kaRne dE bee-ye?]

Are there day passes? weekly passes?
Y a-t-il des cartes pour la journée? pour la semaine?
[ya teel de kaRt pooR la zhooRnay? pooR la sEmen?]

Which direction should I take to get to...?
Quelle direction faut-il prendre pour aller à...?
[kel deeReksyoñ foteel pRañdR pooR alay a...?]

Do I have to transfer?
Est-ce qu'il faut faire une correspondance?
[es keel fo feR Un køRespoñdañs?]

Do you have a map of the subway?
Avez-vous un plan du métro?
[avay voo œñ plañ dU maytRo?]

When is the first subway?
À quelle heure est le premier métro?
[a kel œR e lE pREmyay maytRo?]

When is the last subway?
À quelle heure est le dernier métro?
[a kel œR e lE deRnyay maytRo?]

Driving - *La conduite automobile*

---

here	*ici*	[eesee]
there	*là*	[la]
go ahead / keep going	*avancer*	[avañsay]
back up	*reculer*	[REkUlay]
straight ahead	*tout droit*	[too dRwa]
left	*à gauche*	[a gosh]
right	*à droite*	[a dRwat]
traffic lights	*feux de circulation*	[fœ dE seeRkUlasyoñ]
red light	*feu rouge*	[fœ Roozh]

green light	*feu vert*	[fœ veR]
yellow light	*feu orangé*	[fœ øRañzhay]
at the traffic lights	*aux feux de circulation*	[o fœ dE seeRkUlasyoñ]
intersection	*carrefour*	[kaRfooR]
traffic circle / roundabout	*carrefour giratoire*	[kaRfooR zheeRatwaR]
one way	*sens unique*	[sañs Uneek]
wrong way	*sens interdit*	[sañs eñteRdee]
go / drive three kilometres	*faites trois kilomètres*	[fet tRwa keelometR]
the second on the right	*la deuxième à droite*	[la dœzyem a dRwat]
the first on the left	*la première à gauche*	[la pREmyeR a gosh]
toll highway	*l'autoroute à péage*	[lotoRoot a pay-azh]
dirt road	*route non revêtue*	[Root noñ REvetU]
pedestrian street	*rue piétonne*	[RU pyaytøn]

Car Rental - *La location d'une voiture*

I would like to rent a car
Je voudrais louer une voiture
[zhE voodRe looay Un vwatUR]

Plan - Map

Do you have an automatic (transmission)?
Vous en avez à transmission automatique?
[voo zañ avay a tRañsmeesyoñ otomateek?]

Do you have a manual (transmission)?
Vous en avez à embrayage manuel?
[voo zañ avay a añbRe-yazh manUel?]

How much is it for one day?
Quel est le tarif pour une journée?
[kel e IE taReef pooR Un zhooRnay?]

How much is it for one week?
Quel est le tarif pour une semaine?
[kel e IE taReef pooR Un sEmen?]

Is mileage unlimited?
Est-ce que le kilométrage est illimité?
[es kE IE keelomaytRazh e teeleemeetay?]

How much is the insurance?
Combien coûte l'assurance?
[koñbyeñ koot lasURañs?]

Is there a deductible for collisions?

Y a-t-il une franchise collision?

[ya teel Un fRañsheez køleezyoñ?]

I have a reservation

J'ai une réservation

[zhay Un RayzeRvasyoñ]

I have a confirmed rate from the head office

J'ai un tarif confirmé par le siège social

[zhay œñ taReef koñfeeRmay paR lE syezh sosyal]

Mechanics - *La mécanique*

air conditioning	*climatisation*	kleemateezasyoñ
antenna	*antenne*	[añten]
antifreeze	*antigel*	[añteezhel]
brakes	*freins*	[fReñ]
bumper	*pare-chocs*	[paRshøk]
cassette	*cassette*	[kaset]
clutch	*embrayage*	[añbRe-yazh]
defroster	*dégivreur*	[dayzheevRER]
diesel	*diesel*	[dyayzel]
fan	*ventilateur*	[vañteelatER]
front (rear) door	*portière avant (arrière)*	[pøRtyeR avañ (aRyeR)]
fuses	*fusibles*	[fUzeebl]

61

gas	*essence*	[esañs]
gear shift	*levier de vitesses*	[lEvyay dE veetes]
glove compartment	*boîte à gants*	[bwat a gañ]
hand brake	*frein à main*	[fReñ a meñ]
hazard lights	*feux de détresse*	[fœ dE daytRes]
headlight	*phare*	[faR]
heater	*chauffage*	[shofazh]
horn	*avertisseur*	[aveRteesER]
key	*clé*	[klay]
lock	*serrure*	[seRUR]
oil	*huile*	[Ueel]
oil filter	*filtre à huile*	[feeltR a Ueel]
pedal	*pédale*	[paydal]
power windows	*glaces électriques*	[glas aylektreek]
radiator	*radiateur*	[Radee-atER]
radio	*radio*	[Radyo]
rear-view mirror	*rétroviseur*	[RaytRoveezER]
seat	*siège*	[syezh]
starter	*démarreur*	[daymaRER]
steering wheel	*volant*	[vølañ]
sunroof	*toit ouvrant*	[twa oovRañ]
tire	*pneu*	[pnœ]
trunk	*coffre arrière*	[køfR aRyeR]
turn signal	*clignotant*	[kleegñøtañ]
unleaded gas	*essence sans plomb*	[esañs sañ ploñ]

warning light	*témoin lumineux*	[tay-mweñ lUmeenœ]
water	*eau*	[o]
windshield	*pare-brise*	[paRbReez]
windshield wiper	*essuie-glace*	[esUeeglas]
antenne	antenna	[añten]
antigel	antifreeze	[añteezhel]
avertisseur	horn	[aveRteesER]
boîte à gants	glove compartment	[bwat a gañ]
cassette	cassette	[kaset]
chauffage	heater	[shofazh]
clé	key	[klay]
clignotant	turn signal	[kleegñøtañ]
climatisation	air conditioning	kleemateezasyoñ
coffre arrière	trunk	[køfR aRyeR]
dégivreur	defroster	[dayzheevRER]
démarreur	starter	[daymaRER]
diesel	diesel	[dyayzel]
eau	water	[o]
embrayage	clutch	[añbRe-yazh]
essence	gas	[esañs]
essence sans plomb	unleaded gas	[esañs sañ ploñ]
essuie-glace	windshield wiper	[esUeeglas]
feux de détresse	hazard lights	[fœ dE daytRes]
filtre à huile	oil filter	[feeltR a Ueel]

63

frein à main	hand brake	[fReñ a meñ]
freins	brakes	[fReñ]
fusibles	fuses	[fUzeebl]
glaces électriques	electric windows	[glas aylektreek]
huile	oil	[Ueel]
levier de vitesses	gear shift	[lEvyay dE veetes]
pare-brise	windshield	[paRbReez]
pare-chocs	bumper	[paRshøk]
pédale	pedal	[paydal]
phare	headlight	[faR]
pneu	tire	[pnœ]
portière avant (arrière)	front (rear) door	[pøRtyeR avañ (aRyeR)]
radiateur	radiator	[Radee-atER]
radio	radio	[Radyo]
rétroviseur	rear-view mirror	[RaytRoveezER]
serrure	lock	[seRUR]
siège	seat	[syezh]
témoin lumineux	warning light	[tay-mweñ lUmeenœ]
toit ouvrant	sunroof	[twa oovRañ]
ventilateur	fan	[vañteelatER]
volant	steering wheel	[vølañ]

Filling up - *Faire le plein*

Fill it up, please
Le plein, s'il vous plaît
[IE pleñ, seel voo ple]

Put in ten dollars' worth
Mettez-en pour dix dollars
[metay zañ pooR dee dolaR]

Could you check the tire pressure, please?
Pourriez-vous vérifier la pression des pneus, s'il vous plaît?
[pooRyay voo vayReefyay la pResyoñ de pnœ, seel voo ple?]

Do you take credit cards?
Acceptez-vous les cartes de crédit?
[akseptay voo le kaRt dE kRaydee?]

HEALTH - *SANTÉ*

hospital	*hôpital*	[opeetal]
pharmacy / drugstore	*pharmacie*	[faRmasee]
doctor	*médecin*	[maydseñ]
dentist	*dentiste*	[dañteest]

65

It hurts here... / My... hurts	J'ai mal...	[zhay mal]
abdomen	à l'abdomen	[a labdømen]
teeth	aux dents	[o dañ]
back	au dos	[o do]
throat	à la gorge	[a la gøRzh]
foot	au pied	[o pyay]
head	à la tête	[a la tet]
stomach	au ventre	[o vañtRE]

I am constipated

Je suis constipé

[zhE sUee koñsteepay]

I have diarrhea

J'ai la diarrhée

[zhay la dyaRay]

I have a fever

Je fais de la fièvre

[zhE fe dla fyevR]

My child has a fever

Mon enfant fait de la fièvre

[moñ añfañ fe dla fyevR]

I have the flu
J'ai la grippe
[zhay la gReep]

I would like to refill this prescription
Je voudrais renouveler cette ordonnance
[zhE voodRe Renoovlay set øRdønañs]

Do you have medication for...
Avez-vous des médicaments contre...
[avay voo de maydeekamañ koñtR...]

headache?
le mal de tête?
[lE mal dE tet?]

the flu?
la grippe
[la gReep?]

I would like...
Je voudrais...
[zhE voodRe...]

birth control pills
des anovulants
[de zanovUlañ?]

condoms
des préservatifs
[de pRayzeRvateef]

sunblock
de la crème solaire
[dE la kRem søleR]

insect repellent
un insectifuge
[œñ eñsekteefUzh]

insect bite cream
du baume pour les piqûres d'insecte
[dU bom pooR le peekUR deñsekt]

malaria pills
des médicaments contre la malaria
[de maydeekamañ koñtRE la malarya]

cleaning (soaking) solution for soft (hard) contact
lenses
*une solution nettoyante (mouillante) pour verres
de contact souples (rigides)*
[Un sølUsyoñ netwayañt (mooyañt) pooR veR dE
koñtakt soopl (reezheed)]

an eyewash
un collyre
[œñ køleeR]

EMERGENCIES - *URGENCES*

Fire!
Au feu!
[o fœ!]

Help!
Au secours!
[o sEkooR!]

Stop thief!
Au voleur!
[o vølœR!]

Please call the police
S'il vous plaît, appelez la police
[seel voo ple, aplay la pølees]

Please call an ambulance
S'il vous plaît, appelez une ambulance
[seel voo ple, aplay Un añbUlañs]

Where is the hospital?
Où est l'hôpital?
[oo e lopeetal?]

Please take me/him/her to the hospital
S'il vous plaît, emmenez-moi/le/la à l'hôpital
[seel voo ple, añmnay mwa/lE/la a lopeetal]

I was attacked
On m'a agressé
[oñ ma agResay]

I was robbed
On m'a volé
[oñ ma vølay]

Our luggage was stolen from the car
On a volé nos bagages dans la voiture
[oñ a vølay no bagazh dañ la vwatUR]

My wallet was stolen
On a volé mon portefeuille
[oñ a vølay moñ pøRtEfE-y]

They had a weapon
Ils avaient une arme
[eel zave Un aRm]

They had a knife
Ils avaient un couteau
[eel zave œñ kooto]

They had a gun
Ils avaient un pistolet
[eel zave œñ peestøle]

MONEY - *ARGENT*

| bank | *banque* | [bañk] |
| exchange bureau | *bureau de change* | [bURo dE shañzh] |

What is the exchange rate for the... Canadian dollar?
Quel est le taux de change pour le... dollar canadien?
[kel e IE to dE shañzh pooR IE... dolaR kanadyeñ?]

American dollar?
dollar américain?
[dolaR amayReekeñ?]

French franc?
franc français?
[fRañ fRañse?]

Belgian franc?
franc belge?
[fRañ belzh?]

Swiss franc?
franc suisse?
[fRañ sUees?]

pound sterling?
livre sterling?
[leevRE steRling?]

I would like to exchange American dollars (Canadian dollars)
Je voudrais changer des dollars américains (canadiens)
[zhE voodRe shañzhay de dolaR amayReekeñ (kanadyeñ)]

I would like to change some traveller's cheques
Je voudrais changer des chèques de voyage
[zhE voodRe shañzhay de shek dE vwayazh]

I would like to get a cash advance on my credit card

Je voudrais obtenir une avance de fonds sur ma carte de crédit

[zhE voodRe øbtEneeR Un avañs dE foñ sUR ma kaRt dE kRaydee]

Where can I find an automatic teller machine (a bank machine)?

Où peut-on trouver un guichet automatique (un distributeur de billets)?

[oo pœtoñ tRoovay œñ geeshe otomateek (œñ deestReebUtER dE bee-ye)?]

MAIL AND TELEPHONE
POSTE ET TÉLÉPHONE

stamps	*timbres*	[teñbR]
weight	*poids*	[pwa]
air mail	*par avion*	[paR avyoñ]
express mail	*courrier rapide*	[kooRyay Rapeed]

Where is the post office?

Où se trouve le bureau de poste?

[oo sE tRoov lE bURo dE pøst?]

How much is it to mail a postcard to Canada / the United States?

Combien coûte l'affranchissement d'une carte postale pour le Canada / les États-Unis?

[koñbyeñ koot lafRañsheesmañ dUn kaRt pøstal pooR IE kanada / le zayta zUnee?]

How much is it to mail a letter to Canada?

Combien coûte l'affranchissement d'une lettre pour le Canada?

[koñbyeñ koot lafRañsheesmañ dUn letR pooR IE kanada?]

Where is the nearest phone booth?

Où est le téléphone public le plus proche?

[oo e IE taylayføn pUbleek IE plU pRøsh?]

How do I make a local call?

Que faut-il faire pour placer un appel local?

[kE foteel feR pooR plasay œñ apel løkal?]

How do I call Canada?

Que faut-il faire pour appeler au Canada?

[kE foteel feR pooR aplay o kanada?]

I would like to buy a telephone card
Je voudrais acheter une carte de téléphone
[zhE voodRe ashtay Un kaRt dE taylayføn]

I would like some change to make a telephone call
J'aimerais avoir de la monnaie pour téléphoner
[zhemRe avwaR dE la møne pooR taylayfønay]

How are telephone calls billed at the hotel?*
Comment les appels sont-ils facturés à l'hôtel?
[kømañ le zapel soñ teel faktURay a lotel?]
*They generally cost two or three times more than those made from a phone booth.

I am calling Canada Direct, it's a toll-free call
J'appelle Canada Direct, c'est un appel sans frais
[zhapel kanada deeRekt, se tœñ apel sañ fRe]

I would like to make a person-to-person call
Je voudrais faire un appel de personne à personne
[zhE voodRe feR œñ apel dE peRsøn a peRsøn]

I would like to send a fax
Je voudrais envoyer un fax
[zhE voodRe añvwa-yay œñ fax]

Have you received a fax for me?
Avez-vous reçu un fax pour moi?
[avay voo REsU œñ fax pooR mwa?]

ELECTRICITY - *ÉLECTRICITÉ*

Where can I plug my razor in?
Où puis-je brancher mon rasoir?
[oo pUeezh bRañshay moñ RazwaR?]

Is the current 220 volts?
L'alimentation est-elle de 220 volts?
[laleemañtasyoñ etel dE dœ sañ veñ vølt?]

The light does not work
La lampe ne fonctionne pas
[la lañp nE foñksyøn pa]

Where can I find batteries for my alarm clock?
Où puis-je trouver des piles pour mon réveil-matin?
[oo pUeezh tRoovay de peel pooR moñ Rayve-y mateñ?]

Could I plug my computer in here?
Est-ce que je peux brancher mon ordinateur ici?
[es kE zhE pœ bRañshay moñ øRdeenatER eesee?]

Is there a telephone jack for my computer?

Y a-t-il une prise téléphonique pour mon ordinateur?

[ya teel Un pReez taylayføneek pooR moñ øRdeenatER?]

WEATHER - *MÉTÉO*

rain	*la pluie*	[la plUee]
sun	*le soleil*	[lE søle-y]
wind	*le vent*	[lE vañ]
snow	*la neige*	[la nezh]
It's hot out	*Il fait chaud*	[eel fe sho]
It's cold out	*Il fait froid*	[eel fe fRwa]
sunny	*ensoleillé*	[añsøle-yay]
cloudy	*nuageux*	[nUazhœ]
rainy	*pluvieux*	[plUvyœ]
la pluie	rain	[la plUee]
le soleil	sun	[lE søle-y]
le vent	wind	[lE vañ]
la neige	snow	[la nezh]
Il fait chaud	It's hot out	[eel fe sho]
Il fait froid	It's cold out	[eel fe fRwa]
ensoleillé	sunny	[añsøle-yay]
nuageux	cloudy	[nUazhœ]
pluvieux	rainy	[plUvyœ]

ELECTRICITY

What is the weather going to be like today?
Quel temps fera-t-il aujourd'hui?
[kel tañ fERa teel ozhooRdUee?]

It's beautiful out!
Comme il fait beau!
[køm eel·fe bo!]

What great weather!
Quelle belle température!
[kel bel tañpayRatUR!]

It's awful out!
Comme il fait mauvais!
[køm eel fe move!]

What terrible weather!
Quel mauvais temps!
[kel move tañ!]

Is it raining?
Est-ce qu'il pleut?
[es keel plœ?]

Will it rain?
Va-t-il pleuvoir?
[va teel plœvwaR?]

Is rain forecasted?
Prévoit-on de la pluie?
[pRayvwa toñ dE la plUee?]

EXPLORING
ATTRAITS TOURISTIQUES

airport	*aéroport*	[a-ayRopøR]
amusement park	*parc d'attractions*	[paRk datRaksyoñ]
archaeological site	*site archéologique*	[seet aRkay- oløzheek]
beach	*plage*	[plazh]
bridge	*pont*	[poñ]
building	*édifice*	[aydeefees]
bus station	*gare routière*	[gaR RootyeR]
cablecar	*téléférique*	[taylayfayReek]
cathedral	*cathédrale*	[kataydRal]
church	*église*	[aygleez]
city hall	*hôtel de ville*	[otel dE veel]
court house	*Palais de justice*	[pale dzhUstees]
fort	*fort*	[føR]

fortress	*forteresse*	[føRtEres]
fountain	*fontaine*	[foñten]
funicular railway	*funiculaire*	[fUneekUleR]
harbour	*port*	[pøR]
historic centre	*centre historique*	[sañtRE eestøReek]
house	*maison*	[mayzoñ]
manor	*manoir*	[manwaR]
marina	*marina*	[maReena]
market	*marché*	[maRshay]
monastery	*monastère*	[mønasteR]
monument	*monument*	[mønUmañ]
museum	*musée*	[mUzay]
old port	*vieux port*	[vyœ pøR]
park	*parc*	[paRk]
pool	*piscine*	[peeseen]
port	*port*	[pøR]
promenade	*promenade*	[pRømnad]
pyramid	*pyramide*	[peeRameed]
river	*rivière / fleuve*	[ReevyeR / flEv]
ruins	*ruines*	[RUeen]
sea	*mer*	[meR]
shopping centre	*centre commercial*	[sañtRE kømeRsyal]
stadium	*stade*	[stad]
statue	*statue*	[statU]
temple	*temple*	[tañpl]

theatre	*théâtre*	[tay-atR]
theme park	*parc d'attractions*	[paRk datRaksyoñ]
train station	*gare ferroviaire*	[gaR feRøvyeR]
tunnel	*tunnel*	[tUnel]
waterfall	*cascade / chute*	[kaskad / shUt]
zoo	*zoo*	[zoo]
aéroport	airport	[a-ayRopøR]
cascade / chute	waterfall	[kaskad / shUt]
cathédrale	cathedral	[kataydRal]
centre commercial	shopping centre	[sañtRE kømeRsyal]
centre historique	historic centre	[sañtRE eestøReek]
édifice	building	[aydeefees]
église	church	[aygleez]
funiculaire	funicular railway	[fUneekUleR]
forteresse	fortress	[føRtEres]
fontaine	fountain	[foñten]
fort	fort	[føR]
gare ferroviaire	train station	[gaR feRøvyeR]
gare routière	bus station	[gaR RootyeR]
hôtel de ville	city hall	[otel dE veel]
maison	house	[mayzoñ]
manoir	manor	[manwaR]
marché	market	[maRshay]
marina	marina	[maReena]

mer	sea	[meR]
monastère	monastery	[mønasteR]
monument	monument	[mønUmañ]
musée	museum	[mUzay]
Palais de justice	court house	[pale dzhUstees]
parc	park	[paRk]
parc d'attractions	amusement park / theme park	[paRk datRaksyoñ]
piscine	pool	[peeseen]
plage	beach	[plazh]
pont	bridge	[poñ]
port	port / harbour	[pøR]
promenade	promenade	[pRømnad]
pyramide	pyramid	[peeRameed]
rivière / fleuve	river	[ReevyeR / flEv]
ruines	ruins	[RUeen]
site archéologique	archaeological site	[seet aRkay-oløzheek]
stade	stadium	[stad]
statue	statue	[statU]
téléférique	cablecar	[taylayfayReek]
temple	temple	[tañpl]
théâtre	theatre	[tay-atR]
tunnel	tunnel	[tUnel]
vieux centre	old centre	[vyœ sañtRE]

vieux port	historic port	[vyœ pøR]
zoo	zoo	[zoo]

Where is downtown?
Où se trouve le centre-ville?
[oo sE tRoov lE sañtRE-veel?]

Where is the historic part of town?
Où se trouve la vieille ville?
[oo sE tRoov la vye-y veel?]

Can I walk there from here?
Peut-on marcher jusque-là?
[pœtoñ maRshay zhUskE la?]

What is the best route to get to...?
Quel est le meilleur chemin pour se rendre à...?
[kel e lE me-yER shEmeñ pooR sE rañdR a...?]

What is the best way to get to...?
Quelle est la meilleure façon de se rendre à...?
[kel e la me-yER fasoñ dE sE rañdR a...?]

How long will it take?
Il faudra combien de temps?
[eel fodRa koñbyeñ dE tañ?]

How much time does it take to get to...?
Combien de temps faut-il pour se rendre à...?
[koñbyeñ de tañ foteel pooR sE rañdR a...?]

Where do I catch the bus for downtown?
Où prend-on le bus pour le centre-ville?
[oo pRañ toñ lE bUs pooR lE sañtRE-veel?]

Is there a subway station near here?
Y a-t-il une station de métro près d'ici?
[ya teel Un stasyoñ dE maytRo pRe deesee?]

Can you go to... by subway?
Peut-on aller à... en métro?
[pœtoñ alay a... añ maytRo?]

Can you go to... by bus?
Peut-on aller à... en bus?
[pœtoñ alay a... añ bUs?]

How much does a bus ticket cost?
Combien coûte un ticket de bus?
[koñbyeñ koot œñ teeke dE bUs?]

How much does a subway ticket cost?
Combien coûte un ticket de métro?
[koñbyeñ koot œñ teeke dE maytRo?]

Do you have a city map?
Avez-vous un plan de la ville?
[avay voo œñ plañ dE la veel?]

I would like a map with an index
Je voudrais un plan avec index
[zhE voodRe œñ plañ avek eñdeks]

At the Museum - *Au musée*

19th century	*XIXe siècle*	[deeznœvyem syekl]
20th century	*XXe siècle*	[veñtyem syekl]
African art	*art africain*	[aR afReekeñ]
American Revolution (U.S.)	*guerre de l'Indépendance*	[geR dE leñdaypañdañs]
anthropology	*anthropologie*	[añtRopoløzhee]
antiques	*antiquités*	[añteekeetay]
archaeology	*archéologie*	[aRkay-oløzhee]
architecture	*architecture*	[aRsheetektUR]
Art Deco	*Art déco*	[aR dayko]
Art Nouveau	*Art nouveau*	[aR noovo]
Asian art	*art asiatique*	[aR azeeateek]
Civil War (U.S.)	*guerre de Sécession*	[geR dE saysesyoñ]
Colonial art	*art colonial*	[aR kølønyal]
colonial wars	*guerres coloniales*	[geR kølønyal]

colonization	*colonisation*	[køløneezasyoñ]
contemporary art	*art contemporain*	[aR koñtañpøReñ]
decorative arts	*arts décoratifs*	[aR daykøRateef]
impressionism	*impressionnisme*	[eñpResyøneesm]
modern art	*art moderne*	[aR mødeRn]
natural sciences	*sciences naturelles*	[syañs natURel]
Native American art	*art amérindien*	[aR amayReñdyeñ]
Northerners	*nordistes*	[nøRdeest]
paintings	*peintures*	[peñtUR]
permanent collection	*collection permanente*	[køleksyoñ peRmanañt]
pre-Columbian art	*art précolombien*	[aR pRaykøloñbyeñ]
sculptures	*sculptures*	[skUltUR]
Southerners	*sudistes*	[sUdeest]
Spanish period	*période hispanique*	[payRyød eespaneek]
temporary exhibition	*exposition temporaire*	[ekspozeesyoñ tañpøReR]
urbanism	*urbanisme*	[URbaneesm]
war of independence	*guerre d'indépendance*	[geR deñdaypañdañs]

anthropologie	anthropology	[añtRopoløzhee]
antiquités	antiques	[añteekeetay]
archéologie	archaeology	[aRkay-oløzhee]
architecture	architecture	[aRsheetektUR]

art africain	African art	[aR afReekeñ]
art asiatique	Asian art	[aR azeeateek]
art amérindien	Native American art	[aR amayReñdyeñ]
art précolombien	pre-Columbian art	[aR praykøloñbyeñ]
art colonial	Colonial art	[aR kølønyal]
Art déco	Art Deco	[aR dayko]
Art nouveau	Art Nouveau	[aR noovo]
art contemporain	contemporary art	[aR koñtañpøReñ]
art moderne	modern art	[aR mødeRn]
arts décoratifs	decorative arts	[aR daykøRateef]
collection permanente	permanent collection	[køleksyoñ peRmanañt]
colonisation	colonization	[køløneezasyoñ]
exposition temporaire	temporary exhibition	[ekspozeesyoñ tañpøReR]
guerre de Sécession	Civil War (U.S.)	[geR dE saysesyoñ]
guerre de l'Indépendance	American Revolution (U.S.)	[geR dE leñdaypañdañs]
guerre d'indépendance	war of independence	[geR deñdaypañdañs]
guerres coloniales	colonial wars	[geR kølønyal]
impressionnisme	impressionism	[eñpResyøneesm]
nordistes	Northerners	[nøRdeest]
peintures	paintings	[peñtUR]
période hispanique	Spanish period	[payRyød eespaneek]

sciences naturelles	natural sciences	[syañs natURel]
sculptures	sculptures	[skUltUR]
sudistes	Southerners	[sUdeest]
urbanisme	urbanism	[URbaneesm]
XIXᵉ siècle	19th century	[deeznœvyem syekl]
XXᵉ siècle	20th century	[veñtyem syekl]

What is the admission fee?
Combien coûte l'entrée?
[koñbyeñ koot lañtRay?]

Is there a student rate?
Y a-t-il un tarif étudiant?
[ya teel œñ taReef aytUdyañ?]

Do children have to pay?
Les enfants doivent-ils payer?
[le zañfañ dwav teel pe-yay?]

What is the museum schedule?
Quel est l'horaire du musée?
[kel e løReR dU mUzay?]

Do you have any reading material on the museum?
Avez-vous de la documentation sur le musée?
[avay voo dE la døkUmañtasyoñ sUR lE mUzay?]

Is it permitted to take photographs?
Est-il permis de prendre des photos?
[eteel peRmee dE pRañdR de foto?]

Where is the coat check?
Où se trouve le vestiaire?
[oo sE tRoov lE vestyeR?]

Is there a cafeteria?
Y a-t-il une cafétéria?
[ya teel Un kafaytayrya?]

Is there a café?
Y a-t-il un café?
[ya teel œñ kafay?]

Where is the painting by...?
Où se trouve le tableau de...?
[oo sE tRoov lE tablo dE...?]

What time does the museum close?
À quelle heure ferme le musée?
[a kel œR feRm lE mUzay?]

Where can I...

Où peut-on pratiquer...

[oo pœtoñ pRateekay ...]

play badminton?	*le badminton?*	[lE badmeentøn]
go bicycling?	*le vélo?*	[lE vaylo]
go cross-country skiing?	*le ski de fond?*	[lE skee dE foñ]
go diving?	*le plongeon?*	[le ploñzhoñ]
go downhill skiing?	*le ski alpin?*	[lE skee alpeñ]
go fishing?	*la pêche?*	[la pesh]
play golf?	*le golf?*	[lE gølf]
go hang-gliding?	*le parapente?*	[lE parapañt]
go hiking?	*la randonnée pédestre?*	[la rañdønay paydestR]
go horseback riding?	*l'équitation?*	[laykeetasyoñ]
jet-ski?	*la motomarine?*	[la motomaReen]
go mountain biking?	*le vélo de montagne?*	[lE vaylo dE moñtagñ]
ride a motorcycle?	*la moto?*	[la moto]
go parachuting?	*le parachutisme?*	[lE paRashUteesm]
go rock climbing?	*l'escalade?*	[leskalad]

go scuba diving?	*la plongée?*	[la ploñzhay]
go snorkelling?	*la plongée-tuba?*	[la ploñzhay tUba]
go snowmobiling?	*la motoneige?*	[la motonezh]
go sport fishing?	*la pêche sportive?*	[la pesh spøRteev]
go swimming?	*la natation?*	[la natasyoñ]
play tennis?	*le tennis?*	[IE tenees]
play volleyball?	*le volley-ball?*	[IE vølay-bøl]
go windsurfing?	*la planche à voile?*	[la plañsh a vwal]

air mattress	*matelas pneumatique*	[matla pnœmateek]
ball	*balle, ballon*	[bal], [baloñ]
beach	*plage*	[plazh]
boat	*bateau*	[bato]
boots	*bottines*	[bøteen]
bicycle	*bicyclette*	[beeseeklet]
cabin	*cabine*	[kabeen]
calm sea	*mer calme*	[meR kalm]
currents	*courants*	[kooRañ]
dangerous currents	*courants dangereux*	[kooRañ dañzhERœ]
deck chair	*chaise longue*	[shez loñg]
fins	*palmes*	[palm]
fishing rod	*canne à pêche*	[kan a pesh]
golf clubs	*bâtons de golf*	[batoñ dE gølf]
high tide	*marée haute*	[maRay ot]

lifeguard	*surveillant*	[sURve-yañ]
low tide	*marée basse*	[maRay bas]
mask	*masque*	[mask]
net	*filet*	[feele]
parasol	*parasol*	[paRasøl]
racket	*raquette*	[Raket]
rock	*rocher*	[Røshay]
rough sea	*mer agitée*	[meR azheetay]
sailboat	*voilier*	[vwalyay]
sand	*sable*	[sablE]
ski poles	*bâtons*	[batoñ]
skis	*skis*	[skee]
surf board	*planche de surf*	[plañsh dE sœRf]
tank	*bonbonne*	[boñbøn]
tennis	*tennis*	[tenees]
windsurfer	*planche à voile*	[plañsh a vwal]

ACCOMMODATIONS
HÉBERGEMENT

single room	*chambre pour une personne*	[shañbR pooR Un peRsøn]
double room	*chambre pour deux personnes*	[shañbR pooR dœ peRsøn]
room for three people	*chambre pour trois personnes*	[shañbR pooR tRwa peRsøn]

apartment-hotel	*hôtel-appartement (résidence hôtelière)*	[otel (rayzidañs otElyeR)]
air conditioning	*la climatisation*	[la kleemateezasyoñ]
baby	*bébé*	[baybay]
balcony	*balcon*	[balkoñ]
bar	*bar*	[baR]
double bed	*lit deux places*	[lee dœ plas]
twin beds	*lits jumeaux*	[lee zhUmo]
sofa-bed	*divan-lit*	[deevañ lee]
bedspread	*couvre-lit*	[koovRElee]
blanket	*couverture*	[kooveRtUR]
blind	*store*	[støR]
blow-dryer	*sèche-cheveux*	[sesh shEvœ]
boutiques	*boutique*	[booteek]
chair	*chaise*	[shez]
child	*enfant*	[añfañ]
coffeemaker	*cafetière*	[kafEtyeR]
corkscrew	*tire-bouchon*	[teeR-booshoñ]
cutlery	*couverts*	[kooveR]
curtains	*rideaux*	[Reedo]
dishes	*vaisselle*	[vaysel]
dishwasher	*lave-vaisselle*	[lav vaysel]
fan	*ventilateur*	[vañteelatœR]
fax machine	*télécopieur*	[taylaykøpyœR]
freezer	*congélateur*	[koñzhaylatœR]
heating	*le chauffage*	[lE shofazh]

ACCOMMODATIONS

ice cube	*glaçon*	[glasoñ]
iron	*fer à repasser*	[feR a REpasay]
ironing board	*planche à repasser*	[plañsh a REpasay]
kitchenette	*cuisinette*	[kUeezeenet]
light / lamp	*lumière*	[lUmyeR]
microwave oven	*four à micro-ondes*	[fooR a meekRo oñd]
mini-bar	*minibar*	[meeneebaR]
noise	*bruit*	[bRUee]
noisy	*bruyant*	[bRUee-yañ]
pillow	*oreiller*	[øRe-yay]
pillowcase	*taie d'oreiller*	[te døRe-yay]
pool	*piscine*	[peeseen]
privacy	*intimité*	[eñteemeetay]
purified water	*eau purifiée*	[o pURefyay]
quiet	*calme*	[kalm]
radio	*radio*	[Radyo]
refrigerator	*réfrigérateur*	[RayfReezhay-RatœR]
restaurant	*restaurant*	[RestoRañ]
room	*chambre*	[shañbRE]
with bathroom	*avec salle de bain*	[avek sal dE beñ]
with bathtub	*avec baignoire*	[avek bengwaR]
with shower	*avec douche*	[avek doosh]
safe	*coffre de sécurité*	[køfRE dE saykUReetay]
sheet	*drap*	[dRa]

soap	*savon*	[savoñ]
stores	*boutiques*	[booteek]
studio	*studio*	[stUdyo]
suite	*suite*	[sUeet]
table	*table*	[table]
tablecloth	*nappe*	[nap]
telephone	*téléphone*	[taylayføn]
television	*télévision*	[taylayveezyoñ]
television set	*téléviseur*	[taylayveezœR]
English channel	*chaîne anglaise*	[shen añglez]
French channel	*chaîne française*	[shen fRañsez]
towel	*serviette*	[seRvyet]
view of	*vue sur*	[vU sUR]
the sea	*la mer*	[la meR]
the city	*la ville*	[la veel]
the mountain	*la montagne*	[la moñtang]
washing machine	*lave-linge*	[lav leñzh]
window	*fenêtre*	[fEnetR]

Do you have a room free for tonight?
Avez-vous une chambre libre pour cette nuit?
[avay voo Un shañbRE leebRE pooR set nUee?]

How much is the room?
Quel est le prix de la chambre?
[kel e lE pRee dE la shañbRE?]

Is tax included?
La taxe est-elle comprise?
[la tax etel koñpReez?]

We would like a room with a bathroom
Nous voulons une chambre avec salle de bain
[noo vooloñ Un shañbRE avek sal dE beñ]

Is breakfast included?
Le petit déjeuner est-il compris?
[lE pEtee dayzhEnay eteel koñpRee?]

Do you have any less expensive rooms?
Avez-vous des chambres moins chères?
[avay voo de shañbRE mweñ sheR?]

Could we see the room?
Pouvons-nous voir la chambre?
[poovoñ noo vwaR la shañbRE?]

I will take it
Je la prends
[zhE la pRañ]

I have a reservation in the name of...
J'ai une réservation au nom de...
[zhay Un RayzeRvasyoñ o noñ dE...]

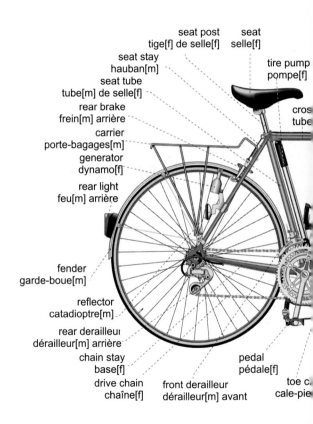

seat post
tige[f] de selle[f]

seat
selle[f]

seat stay
hauban[m]

tire pump
pompe[f]

seat tube
tube[m] de selle[f]

cros
tube

rear brake
frein[m] arrière

carrier
porte-bagages[m]

generator
dynamo[f]

rear light
feu[m] arrière

fender
garde-boue[m]

reflector
catadioptre[m]

rear derailleur
dérailleur[m] arrière

chain stay
base[f]

drive chain
chaîne[f]

front derailleur
dérailleur[m] avant

pedal
pédale[f]

toe c.
cale-pie

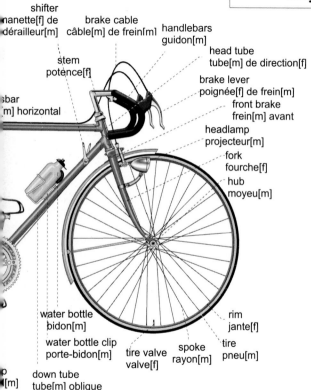

bicyclette[f]
bicycle

shifter
manette[f] de
dérailleur[m]

brake cable
câble[m] de frein[m]

handlebars
guidon[m]

head tube
tube[m] de direction[f]

stem
potence[f]

brake lever
poignée[f] de frein[m]

front brake
frein[m] avant

sbar
m] horizontal

headlamp
projecteur[m]

fork
fourche[f]

hub
moyeu[m]

water bottle
bidon[m]

water bottle clip
porte-bidon[m]

tire valve
valve[f]

spoke
rayon[m]

rim
jante[f]

tire
pneu[m]

p
[m]

down tube
tube[m] oblique

Illustration by Québec/Amérique International © 1992

I have a confirmed rate of...
On m'a confirmé le tarif de...
[oñ ma koñfeeRmay lE taReef dE...]

Do you take credit cards?
Est-ce que vous acceptez les cartes de crédit?
[es kE voo zakseptay lE kaRt dE kRaydee?]

Would it be possible to have a quieter room?
Est-il possible d'avoir une chambre plus calme?
[eteel pøseeblE davwaR Un shañbRE plU kalm?]

Where can we park the car?
Où pouvons-nous garer la voiture?
[oo poovoñ noo gaRay la vwatUR?]

Could someone help us take our bags to the room?
Quelqu'un peut-il nous aider à monter nos bagages?
[kelkœñ pœteel noo zeday a moñtay no bagazh?]

What time do we have to be out of the room?
À quelle heure devons-nous quitter la chambre?
[a kel œR dEvoñ noo keetay la shañbRE?]

Is the tap water drinkable?
Peut-on boire l'eau du robinet?
[pœtoñ bwar lo dU Røbeene?]

When is breakfast served?
À partir de quelle heure peut-on prendre le petit déjeuner?
[a paRteeR dE kel œR pœtoñ pRañdRE lE pEtee
dayzhEnay?]

Could we change our room?
Pourrions-nous changer de chambre?
[pooRyoñ noo shañzhay dE shañbRE?]

We would like a quieter room
Nous voudrions une chambre moins bruyante
[noo voodReeoñ Un shañbRE mweñ bRUee-yañt]

We would like a room with a view of the sea
Nous voudrions une chambre avec vue sur la mer
[noo voodReeoñ Un shañbRE avek vU sUR la meR]

Could we have two keys?
Est-ce que nous pouvons avoir deux clés?
[es kE noo poovoñ avwaR dœ klay?]

Is there...
Y a-t-il...
[ya teel]

a pool?	*une piscine?*	[Un peeseen]
a gym?	*un gymnase?*	[œñ zheemnaz]
a tennis court?	*un court de tennis?*	[œñ kooR dE tenees]
a golf course?	*un terrain de golf?*	[œñ teReñ dE gølf]
a marina?	*une marina?*	[Un maReena]

What time does the pool close?
Jusqu'à quelle heure la piscine est-elle ouverte?
[zhUska kel œR la peeseen etel ooveRt?]

What time does the pool open?
À partir de quelle heure peut-on aller à la piscine?
[a paRteeR dE kel œR pœtoñ alay a la peeseen?]

Where can we get towels for the pool?
Où pouvons-nous prendre des serviettes pour la piscine?
[oo poovoñ noo pRañdRE de seRvyet pooR la peeseen?]

Is there bar service at the pool?
Y a-t-il un service de bar à la piscine?
[ya teel œñ seRvees dE baR a la peeseen?]

When is the gym open?
Quelles sont les heures d'ouverture du gymnase?
[kel soñ le zER dooveRtUR dU zheemnaz?]

Is there a safe in the room?
Y a-t-il un coffre de sécurité dans la chambre?
[ya teel œñ køfRE dE saykUReetay dañ la shañbRE?]

Could you wake me up at...? (see p 39)
Pouvez-vous me réveiller à...?
[poovay voo mE Rayve-yay a...?]

The air conditioning does not work
La climatisation ne fonctionne pas
[la kleemateezasyoñ nE foñksyøn pa]

The toilet is blocked
La cuvette des toilettes est bouchée
[la kUvet de twalet e booshay]

There is no electricity
Il n'y a pas d'électricité
[eel nya pa daylektReeseetay]

May I have the key to the safe?
Puis-je avoir la clé du coffre de sécurité?
[pUeezh avwaR la klay dU køfRE dE saykUReetay?]

The telephone does not work
Le téléphone ne fonctionne pas
[lE taylayføn nE foñksyøn pa]

Do you have any messages for me?

Avez-vous des messages pour moi?

[avay voo de mesazh pooR mwa?]

Have you received a fax for me?

Avez-vous reçu un fax pour moi?

[avay voo REsU œñ fax pooR mwa]

Could you call us a taxi?

Pouvez-vous nous appeler un taxi?

[poovay voo noo aplay œñ taksee?]

Could you call us a taxi for tomorrow morning at 6am?

Pouvez-vous nous appeler un taxi pour demain à 6 h?

[poovay voo noo aplay œñ taksee pooR dEmeñ a see zœR]

We are leaving now

Nous partons maintenant

[noo paRtoñ meñtnañ]

Could you get the bill ready?

Pouvez-vous préparer la note?

[poovay voo pRaypaRay la noT?]

I think there is a mistake on the bill.
Je crois qu'il y a une erreur sur la note.
[zhE kRwa keel ya Un eRœR sUR la noT]

I had a confirmed rate of...
On m'avait garanti le tarif de...
[oñ mave gaRañtee lE taReef dE...]

Could you have our bags brought down?
Pouvez-vous faire descendre nos bagages?
[poovay voo feR desañdRE no bagazh?]

Could you keep our bags until...? (see p 39)
Pouvez-vous garder nos bagages jusqu'à...?
[poovay voo gaRday no bagazh zhUska...?]

Thank you for everything, we have had an excellent stay here
Merci pour tout, nous avons fait un excellent séjour chez vous
[meRsee pooR too, noo zavoñ fe œñ ekselañ sayzhooR shay voo]

We hope to come back soon
Nous espérons revenir bientôt
[noo zespayRoñ REvneeR byeñto]

Mexican cuisine... (see Country, p 44)
La cuisine mexicaine...
[la kUeezeen mekseeken...]

Could you recommend ... restaurant?
Pouvez-vous nous recommander un restaurant...?
[poovay voo noo REkømañday œñ RestoRañ...?]

a Chinese	*chinois*	[sheenwa]
a French	*français*	[fRañse]
an Indian	*indien*	. [eñdyeñ]
an Italian	*italien*	[eetalyeñ]
a Japanese	*japonais*	[zhapøne]
a Mexican	*mexicain*	[mekseekeñ]

I would like to make a reservation for four people for
about 9 p.m.
Je voudrais faire une réservation pour quatre personnes
vers 21 heures
[zhE voodRe feR Un RayzeRvasyoñ pooR katRE peRsøn
veR veñ tay Un œR]

I would like to make a reservation for two people for about 8 p.m.

Je voudrais faire une réservation pour deux personnes vers 20 heures

[zhE voodRe feR Un RayzeRvasyoñ pooR dœ peRsøn veR veñ tœR]

Will you have room later on?

Est-ce que vous aurez de la place plus tard?

[es kE voo zoRay dE la plas plU taR?]

I would like to reserve for tomorrow night

Je voudrais réserver pour demain soir

[zhE voodRe RayzeRvay pooR dEmeñ swaR]

When is the restaurant open?

Quelles sont les heures d'ouverture du restaurant?

[kel soñ le zœR dooveRtUR dU RestoRañ?]

What time does the restaurant open?

À quelle heure le restaurant ouvre-t-il?

[a kel œR lE RestoRañ oovRE teel?]

What time does the restaurant close?

À quelle heure le restaurant ferme-t-il?

[a kel œR lE RestoRañ feRmE teel?]

Do you take credit cards?
Acceptez-vous les cartes de crédit?
[akseptay voo lE kaRtE dE kRaydee?]

I would like to see the menu
J'aimerais voir le menu
[zhemRe vwaR lE mEnU]

Could we just have a drink?
Pouvons-nous simplement prendre un verre?
[poovoñ noo señplEmañ pRañdRE œñ veR?]

Could we just have a coffee?
Pouvons-nous simplement prendre un café?
[poovoñ noo señplEmañ pRañdRE œñ kafay?]

I am vegetarian
Je suis végétarien
[zhE sUee vayzhaytaRyeñ]

I do not eat pork
Je ne mange pas de porc
[zhE nE mañzh pa dE pøR]

I am allergic to nuts
Je suis allergique aux noix
[zhE sUee zaleRzheek o nwa]

I am allergic to eggs
Je suis allergique aux œufs
[zhE sUee zaleRzheek o zœ]

Do you serve wine by the glass?
Servez-vous du vin au verre?
[seRvay voo dU veñ o veR?]

We did not get...
Nous n'avons pas eu...
[noo navoñ pa U...]

I asked for...
J'ai demandé...
[zhay dEmañday...]

It is cold
C'est froid
[se fRwa]

It is too salty
C'est trop salé
[se tRo salay]

It is not fresh
Ce n'est pas frais
[sE ne pa fRe]

The bill / check please
L'addition, s'il vous plaît
[ladeesyoñ, seel voo ple]

Is the tip included?
Le service est-il compris?
[lE seRvees eteel koñpRee?]

Thank you, it was an excellent meal
Merci, ce fut un excellent repas
[meRsee, sE fU tœñ ekselañ REpa]

Thank you, we have had a very pleasant evening
Merci, nous avons passé une très agréable soirée
[meRsee, noo zavoñ pasay Un tRe zagRay-ablE swaRay]

I would like a table...
Je voudrais une table...
[zhE voodRe Un tablE]

on the patio	*sur la terrasse*	[sUR la teRas]
near the window	*près de la fenêtre*	[pRe dE la fEnetRE]
upstairs	*en haut*	[añ o]
downstairs	*en bas*	[añ ba]

dining room	*salle à manger*	[sal a mañzhay]
kitchen	*cuisine*	[kUeezeen]
patio	*terrasse*	[teRas]
washrooms	*toilettes*	[twalet]
table	*table*	[tablE]
window	*fenêtre*	[fEnetRE]
chair	*chaise*	[shez]
booth	*banquette*	[bañket]
breakfast	*petit déjeuner*	[pEtee dayzhEnay]
lunch	*déjeuner*	[dayzhEnay]
dinner / supper	*dîner*	[deenay]
appetizer	*entrée*	[añtRay]
soup	*soupe*	[soop]
dish	*plat*	[pla]
main dish	*plat principal*	[pla pReñseepal]
sandwich	*sandwich*	[sañdweetsh]
salad	*salade*	[salad]
cheese	*fromage*	[fRømazh]
dessert	*dessert*	[dayseR]
aperitif	*apéritif*	[apayReeteef]
coffee chaser	*digestif/ pousse-café*	[deezhesteef/ poos-kafay]
beer	*bière*	[byeR]
wine	*vin*	[veñ]

wine list	*carte des vins*	[kaRtE dE veñ]
local wine	*vin du pays*	[veñ dU pay-ee]
white wine	*vin blanc*	[veñ blañ]
red wine	*vin rouge*	[veñ Roozh]
house wine	*vin maison*	[veñ mayzoñ]
bottle	*bouteille*	[boote-y]
half-bottle	*demi-bouteille*	[dEmee boote-y]
half	*un demi*	[œñ dEmee]
quarter	*un quart*	[œñ kaR]
dry	*sec*	[sek]
sweet	*doux*	[doo]
bubbly / sparkling	*mousseux*	[moosœ]
with ice	*avec glaçons*	[avek glasoñ]
without ice	*sans glaçons*	[sañ glasoñ]
mineral water	*eau minérale*	[o meenayRal]
sparkling mineral water	*eau minérale pétillante*	[o meenayRal paytee-yañt]
flat mineral water	*eau minérale plate*	[o meenayRal plat]
cocoa / hot chocolate	*chocolat chaud*	[shokola sho]
coffee	*café*	[kafay]
coffee with milk	*café avec du lait*	[kafay avek dU le]
cream	*crème*	[kRem]
espresso	*express*	[ekspRes]
juice	*jus*	[zhU]

herbal tea	*tisane*	[teezan]
milk	*lait*	[le]
orange juice	*jus d'orange*	[zhU døRañzh]
soft drink	*boisson gazeuse*	[bwasoñ gazœz]
sugar	*sucre*	[sUkRE]
tea	*thé*	[tay]
salt	*sel*	[sel]
pepper	*poivre*	[pwavRE]
sauce	*sauce*	[sos]
butter	*beurre*	[bœR]
bread	*pain*	[peñ]
spice (see p 122)	*épice*	[aypees]
spicy	*épicé*	[aypeesay]
plate	*assiette*	[asyet]
ashtray	*cendrier*	[sañdRee-ay]
knife	*couteau*	[kooto]
spoon	*cuillère*	[kUee-yeR]
fork	*fourchette*	[fooRshet]
menu	*menu*	[mEnU]
napkin	*serviette de table*	[seRvyet dE tablE]
saucer	*soucoupe*	[sookoop]
cup	*tasse*	[tas]
glass	*verre*	[veR]

vegetarian dishes	*plats végétariens*	[pla vayzhaytaRyeñ]
vegetables (see p 113)	*légumes*	[laygUm]
fruits (see p 126)	*fruits*	[fRUee]
grilled meat / vegetables	*grillades*	[gRee-yad]
fish	*poisson*	[pwasoñ]
seafood	*fruits de mer*	[fRUee dE meR]
poultry	*volaille*	[vøla-y]
meat	*viande*	[vyañd]
offals	*abats*	[aba]
venison	*venaison*	[vEnezoñ]
sausage	*saucisse*	[sosees]
nuts	*noix*	[nwa]
rice	*riz*	[Ree]
rare	*saignant*	[segñañ]
medium rare	*rosé*	[Rozay]
medium	*à point (médium)*	[a pweñ (maydyEm)]
well done	*bien cuit*	[byeñ kUee]
stuffed	*farci*	[faRsee]
raw	*cru*	[kRU]
au gratin	*gratiné*	[gRateenay]
breaded	*pané*	[panay]
baked	*au four*	[o fooR]

RESTAURANTS

111

sauteed	*à la poêle*	[a la pwal]
grilled	*sur le gril*	[sUR lE gReel]
over a wood fire	*sur des charbons de bois*	[sUR de shaRboñ dE bwa]
minced	*émincé*	[aymeñsay]
roasted	*rôti*	[Rotee]
stir fry	*sauté*	[sotay]

Breakfast - *Petit déjeuner*

---

bread	*pain*	[peñ]
cheese	*fromage*	[fRømazh]
soft cheese	*fromage frais (fromage blanc)*	[fRømazh fRe (fRømazh blañ)]
coffee	*café*	[kafay]
crepes	*crêpes*	[kRep]
croissant	*croissant*	[kRwasañ]
eggs	*œufs*	[œ]
French toast	*pain doré (pain perdu)*	[peñ døRay (peñ peRdU)]
fruits (see p 126)	*fruits*	[fRUee]
granola	*granola*	[gRanola]
jam	*confiture*	[koñfeetUR]
jelly	*gelée*	[zhElay]
juice	*jus*	[zhU]
marmalade	*marmelade*	[maRmElad]
muesli	*musli*	[mUslee]

omelette	*omelette*	[ømlet]
pancakes	*crêpes*	[kRep]
pastry	*viennoiserie*	[vyenwazRee]
toast	*toasts*	[tost]
yogurt	*yaourt*	[yaooRt]
waffles	*gaufres*	[gofR]
whole-wheat bread	*pain de blé entier*	[peñ dE blay añtyay]

Vegetables - *Légumes*

---

asparagus	*asperge*	[aspeRzh]
avocado	*avocat*	[avoka]
bean	*fève*	[fev]
broccoli	*brocoli*	[bRøkølee]
Brussels sprouts	*choux de Bruxelles*	[shoo dE bRUsel]
cabbage	*chou*	[shoo]
cactus	*cactus*	[kaktUs]
carrot	*carotte*	[kaRøt]
cauliflower	*chou-fleur*	[shooflœR]
celery	*céleri*	[selRee]
corn	*maïs*	[ma-ees]
cucumber	*concombre*	[koñkoñbRE]
eggplant	*aubergine*	[obeRzheen]
fennel	*fenouil*	[fEnoo‿y]

garlic	*ail*	[a-y]
leek	*poireau*	[pwaro]
lettuce	*laitue*	[letU]
mushroom	*champignon*	[shañpeengoñ]
okra	*ocra*	[okRa]
onion	*oignon*	[ønyoñ]
pea	*pois*	[pwa]
potato	*pomme de terre*	[pøm dE teR]
radish	*radis*	[Radee]
red/hot/chilli pepper	*piment*	[peemañ]
snowpea	*pois mange-tout*	[pwa mañzh-too]
spinach	*épinards*	[aypeenaR]
squash	*courge*	[kooRzh]
string bean	*haricot*	[aReeko]
sweet/bell pepper	*poivron*	[pwavRoñ]
tomato	*tomate*	[tømat]
turnip	*navet*	[nave]
watercress	*cresson*	[kResoñ]
zucchini	*courgette*	[kooRzhet]
ail	garlic	[a-y]
asperge	asparagus	[aspeRzh]
aubergine	eggplant	[obeRzheen]
avocat	avocado	[avoka]
brocoli	broccoli	[bRøkølee]
cactus	cactus	[kaktUs]

114

carotte	carrot	[kaRøt]
céleri	celery	[selRee]
champignon	mushroom	[shañpeengoñ]
chou	cabbage	[shoo]
chou-fleur	cauliflower	[shooflERE]
choux de Bruxelles	Brussels sprouts	[shoo dbRUsel]
concombre	cucumber	[koñkoñbRE]
courge	squash	[kooRzh]
courgette	zucchini	[kooRzhet]
cresson	watercress	[kResoñ]
épinards	spinach	[aypeenaR]
fenouil	fennel	[fEnoo<u>y</u>]
fève	bean	[fev]
haricot	string bean	[aReeko]
laitue	lettuce	[letU]
maïs	corn	[ma-ees]
navet	turnip	[nave]
ocra	okra	[okRa]
oignon	onion	[øñyoñ]
piment	red/hot/chile pepper	[peemañ]
poireau	leek	[pwaro]
pois	pea	[pwa]
pois mange-tout	snowpea	[pwa mañzh-too]
poivron	sweet/bell pepper	[pwavRoñ]
pomme de terre	potato	[pøm dE teR]

radis	radish	[Radee]
tomate	tomato	[tømat]
courgette	zucchini	[kooRzhet]

Meat - *Viandes*

beef	*bœuf*	[bœf]
blood sausage	*boudin*	[boodeñ]
boar	*sanglier*	[sañglee-ay]
brains	*cervelle*	[seRvel]
breast	*poitrine*	[pwatReen]
brochette	*brochette*	[bRøshet]
capon	*chapon*	[shapoñ]
chicken	*poulet*	[poole]
cubes	*cubes*	[kUb]
cutlet	*côtelette*	[kotlet]
deer	*cerf*	[seR]
duck	*canard / magret*	[kanaR / magRe]
escalope	*escalope*	[eskaløp]
feet	*pattes*	[pat]
filet/tenderloin	*filet*	[feele]
goat	*chèvre*	[shevRE]
goose	*oie*	[wa]
grilled	*grillé*	[gRee-yay]
ground	*haché*	[ashay]
ham	*jambon*	[zhañboñ]

hare	*lièvre*	[lyevRE]
kid	*chevreau*	[shEvRo]
kidneys	*rognons*	[røgñoñ]
lamb	*agneau*	[agño]
leg	*cuisse*	[kUees]
liver	*foie*	[fwa]
meat ball	*boulette*	[boolet]
partridge	*perdrix*	[peRdRee]
pork	*porc*	[pøR]
quail	*caille*	[ka-y]
rabbit	*lapin*	[lapeñ]
ribsteak	*entrecôte*	[añtREkot]
shank	*jarret*	[zhaRe]
slice	*tranche*	[tRañsh]
smoked	*fumé*	[fUmay]
steak	*bifteck*	[beeftek]
sweetbreads	*ris*	[Ree]
tartare	*tartare*	[taRtaR]
thigh	*cuisse*	[kUees]
tongue	*langue*	[lañg]
turkey	*dinde*	[deñd]
veal	*veau*	[vo]
agneau	lamb	[agño]
bifteck	steak	[beeftek]
bœuf	beef	[bEf]

117

boudin	blood sausage	[boodeñ]
boulette	meat ball	[boolet]
brochette	brochette	[bRøshet]
caille	quail	[ka-y]
canard	duck	[kanaR]
cerf	deer	[seR]
cervelle	brains	[seRvel]
chapon	capon	[shapoñ]
chèvre	goat	[shevRE]
chevreau	kid	[shEvRo]
côtelette	cutlet	[kotlet]
cubes	cubes	[kUb]
cuisse	thigh / leg	[kUees]
dinde	turkey	[deñd]
entrecôte	ribsteak	[añtREkot]
escalope	escalope	[eskaløp]
filet	filet/tenderloin	[feele]
foie	liver	[fwa]
fumé	smoked	[fUmay]
grillé	grilled	[gRee-yay]
haché	ground	[ashay]
jambon	ham	[zhañboñ]
jarret	shank	[zhaRe]
langue	tongue	[lañg]
lapin	rabbit	[lapeñ]
lièvre	hare	[lyevRE]

magret	duck	[magRe]
oie	goose	[wa]
pattes	feet	[pat]
perdrix	partridge	[peRdRee]
poitrine	breast	[pwatReen]
porc	pork	[pøR]
poulet	chicken	[poole]
ris	sweetbreads	[Ree]
rognons	kidneys	[røgñoñ]
sanglier	boar	[sañglee-ay]
tartare	tartare	[taRtaR]
tranche	slice	[tRañsh]
veau	veal	[vo]

Fish and Seafood
Poissons et fruits de mer

anchovy	*anchois*	[añshwE]
bass	*bar*	[baR]
clams	*palourdes*	[palooRd]
cod	*morue*	[møRU]
crab	*crabe*	[kRab]
eel	*anguille*	[añgee-y]
escargots	*escargots*	[eskaRgo]
filet	*filet*	[feele]
hake	*colin*	[køleñ]
herring	*hareng*	[aRañ]

119

lobster	*homard*	[omaR]
monkfish	*lotte*	[løt]
mullet	*vivaneau*	[veevano]
octopus	*pieuvre / poulpe*	[pyEvRE / poolp]
oyster	*huîtres*	[UeetRE]
ray	*raie*	[Re]
rock lobster	*langouste*	[lañgoost]
salmon	*saumon*	[somoñ]
sardines	*sardines*	[saRdeen]
scallops	*pétoncles*	[paytoñkl]
scampi	*langoustine*	[lañgoosteen]
sea urchin	*oursin*	[ooRseñ]
shark	*requin*	[REkeñ]
shrimp	*crevettes*	[kREvet]
smoked salmon	*saumon fumé*	[somoñ fUmay]
snails	*escargots*	[eskaRgo]
snapper	*rouget*	[Roozhe]
sole	*sole*	[søl]
squid	*calmar*	[kalmaR]
steak	*darne*	[daRn]
striped bass	*loup de mer*	[loo dE meR]
swordfish	*espadon*	[espadoñ]
trout	*truite*	[tRUeet]
tuna	*thon*	[toñ]
turbot	*turbot*	[tURbo]
whiting	*merlan*	[meRlañ]

anchois	anchovy	[añshwa]
anguille	eel	[añgee-y]
bar	bass	[baR]
calmar	squid	[kalmaR]
colin	hake	[køleñ]
crabe	crab	[kRab]
crevettes	shrimp	[kREvet]
darne	(fish) steak	[daRn]
écrevisse	*crawfish*	[aykREvees]
escargots	*snails / escargots*	[eskaRgo]
espadon	*swordfish*	[espadoñ]
filet	filet	[feele]
hareng	herring	[aRañ]
homard	lobster	[omaR]
huîtres	oysters	[UeetR]
langouste	rock lobster	[lañgoost]
langoustine	scampi	[lañgoosteen]
lotte	monkfish	[løt]
loup de mer	striped bass	[loo dE meR]
merlan	whiting	[meRlañ]
morue	cod	[møRU]
oursin	sea urchin	[ooRseñ]
palourdes	clams	[palooRd]
pétoncles	scallops	[paytoñkl]
pieuvre	octopus	[pyEvR]
poulpe	octopus	[poolp]
raie	ray	[Re]

requin	shark	[REkeñ]
rouget	mullet	[Roozhe]
sardines	sardines	[saRdeen]
saumon	salmon	[somoñ]
saumon fumé	smoked salmon	[somoñ fUmay]
sole	sole	[søl]
thon	tuna	[toñ]
truite	trout	[tRUeet]
turbot	turbot	[tURbo]
vivaneau	snapper	[veevano]

Spices, Herbs and Condiments
Épices, herbes et condiments

cinnamon	*cannelle*	[kanel]
coriander	*coriandre*	[køRyañdRE]
curry	*curry*	[kURee]
ginger	*gingembre*	[zheñzhañbRE]
hot mustard	*moutarde forte*	[mootaRd føRt]
ketchup	*ketchup*	[ketshøp]
mint	*menthe*	[mañt]
nutmeg	*muscade*	[mUskad]
pepper	*poivre*	[pwavRE]
pink pepper	*poivre rose*	[pwavRE Roz]
rosemary	*romarin*	[RømaReñ]
sage	*sauge*	[sozh]
sorrel	*oseille*	[oze-y]

soya sauce	*sauce soya*	[sos soya]
sweet / mild mustard	*moutarde douce*	[mootaRd doos]
Tabasco sauce	*sauce Tabasco*	[sos tabasko]
thyme	*thym*	[teñ]
vinegar	*vinaigre*	[veenegRE]
cannelle	cinnamon	[kanel]
coriandre	coriander	[køRyañdRE]
curry	curry	[kURee]
gingembre	ginger	[zheñzhañbRE]
ketchup	ketchup	[ketshøp]
menthe	mint	[mañt]
moutarde douce	sweet / mild mustard	[mootaRd doos]
moutarde forte	hot mustard	[mootaRd føRt]
muscade	nutmeg	[mUskad]
oseille	sorrel	[oze-y]
poivre	(black) pepper	[pwavR]
poivre rose	pink pepper	[pwavRE Roz]
romarin	rosemary	[RømaReñ]
sauce Tabasco	Tabasco sauce	[sos tabasko]
sauce soya	soya sauce	[sos soya]
sauge	sage	[sozh]
thym	thyme	[teñ]
vinaigre	vinegar	[veenegRE]

Taste - *Le goût*

bitter	*amer*	[ameR]
bland	*fade*	[fad]
hot	*épicé*	[aypeesay]
mild	*doux*	[doo]
peppery	*poivré*	[pwavray]
salty	*salé*	[salay]
spicy	*piquant*	[peekañ]
sweet	*sucré*	[sUkRay]
sweet	*doux*	[doo]

amer	bitter	[ameR]
doux	sweet / mild	[doo]
épicé	spicy	[aypeesay]
fade	bland	[fad]
piquant	hot / spicy	[peekañ]
poivré	peppery	[pwavray]
salé	salty	[salay]
sucré	sweet	[sUkRay]

Desserts - *Desserts*

cake	*gâteau*	[gato]
caramel	*caramel*	[kaRamel]

124

chocolate	*chocolat*	[shokola]
chocolate mousse	*mousse au chocolat*	[moos o shokola]
custard	*crème-dessert*	[kRem dayseR]
flan	*flan*	[flañ]
ice cream	*glace (crème glacée)*	[glas (kRem glasay)]
meringue	*meringue*	[meReng]
pastry	*pâtisserie*	[pateesRee]
pie	*tarte*	[taRt]
sorbet	*sorbet*	[søRbe]
vanilla	*vanille*	[vanee-y]

caramel	caramel	[kaRamel]
chocolat	chocolate	[shokola]
crème-dessert	custard	[kRem dayseR]
flan	flan	[flañ]
gâteau	cake	[gato]
glace (crème glacée)	ice cream	[glas (kRem glasay)]
meringue	meringue	[meReng]
mousse au chocolat	chocolate mousse	[moos o shokola]
pâtisserie	pastry	[pateesRee]
sorbet	sorbet	[søRbe]
tarte	pie	[taRt]
vanille	vanilla	[vanee-y]

Fruits - *Fruits*

apple	*pomme*	[pøm]
apricot	*abricot*	[abReeko]
banana	*banane*	[banan]
blackberry	*mûre*	[mUR]
blueberry	*bleuet (myrtille)*	[blœ-e (meeRtee-y)]
carambola	*carambole*	[kaRañbøl]
cherry	*cerise*	[sEReez]
clementine	*clémentine*	[klaymañteen]
coconut	*coco*	[koko]
grape	*raisin*	[Rayzeñ]
grapefruit	*pamplemousse*	[pañplEmoos]
guava	*goyave*	[goyav]
kiwi	*kiwi*	[keewee]
lemon	*citron*	[seetRoñ]
lime	*lime*	[leem]
mandarine	*mandarine*	[mañdaReen]
mango	*mangue*	[mañg]
melon	*melon*	[mEloñ]
morello	*griotte*	[gReeøt]
orange	*orange*	[øRañzh]
papaya	*papaye*	[papa-y]
passionfruit	*fruit de la passion*	[fRUee dE la pasyoñ]

peach	*pêche*	[pesh]
pear	*poire*	[pwaR]
pineapple	*ananas*	[anana]
plantain	*plantain*	[plañteñ]
plum	*prune/mirabelle*	[pRUn/meeRabel]
pomelo	*pomélo*	[pømaylo]
pumpkin	*citrouille (potiron)*	[seetRoo-y (pøteeRoñ)]
raisin	*raisin sec*	[Rayzeñ sek]
raspberry	*framboise*	[fRañbwaz]
soursop	*corossol*	[koRosøl]
star fruit	*carambole*	[kaRañbøl]
strawberry	*fraise*	[fRez]
tangerine	*tangerine*	[tañzhEReen]
abricot	apricot	[abReeko]
ananas	pineapple	[anana]
banane	banana	[banan]
bleuet (myrtille)	blueberry	[blœ-e (meeRtee-y)]
carambole	star fruit/ carambola	[kaRañbøl]
cerise	cherry	[sEReez]
citron	lemon	[seetRoñ]
citrouille (potiron)	pumpkin	[seetRoo-y (pøteeRoñ)]
clémentine	clementine	[klaymañteen]
coco	coconut	[koko]

127

corossol	soursop	[koRosøl]
fraise	strawberry	[fRez]
framboise	raspberry	[fRañbwaz]
fruit de la passion	passionfruit	[fRUee dE la pasyoñ]
goyave	guava	[goyav]
griotte	morello	[gReeøt]
kiwi	kiwi	[keewee]
lime	lime	[leem]
mandarine	mandarine	[mañdaReen]
mangue	mango	[mañg]
melon	melon	[mEloñ]
mirabelle	plum	[meeRabel]
mûre	blackberry	[mUR]
orange	orange	[øRañzh]
pamplemousse	grapefruit	[pañplEmoos]
papaye	papaya	[papa-y]
pêche	peach	[pesh]
plantain	plantain	[plañteñ]
poire	pear	[pwaR]
pomélo	pomelo	[pømaylo]
pomme	apple	[pøm]
prune	plum	[pRUn]
raisin sec	raisin	[Rayzeñ sek]
raisin	grape	[Rayzeñ]
tangerine	tangerine	[tañzhEReen]

Special Events - *Divertissements*

ballet	*ballet*	[bale]
baseball	*baseball*	[bayzbøl]
bullfight	*tauromachie*	[toRomashee]
bullfighter	*toréador*	[toRay-adøR]
cinema	*cinéma*	[seenayma]
concert	*concert*	[koñseR]
folk dance	*danse folklorique*	[dañs følkløReek]
folklore	*folklore*	[følkløR]
football	*football*	[footbøl]
hockey	*hockey*	[økay]
intermission	*intermission*	[eñteRmeesyoñ]
movie theatre	*cinéma*	[seenayma]
opera	*opéra*	[opayRa]
program	*programme*	[pRøgRam]
reserved seat	*siège réservé*	[syezh RayzeRvay]
seat	*siège*	[syezh]
soccer	*soccer*	[søkeR]
show	*spectacle*	[spektaklE]
theatre	*théâtre*	[tay-atRE]

| ticket counter | *billetterie* | [bee-yetRee] |
| ticket office | *guichet* | [geeshe] |

the least expensive seats
les places les moins chères
[le plas le mweñ sheR]

the best seats
les meilleures places
[le me-yœR plas]

I would like ... seats
Je voudrais... places
[zhE voodRe ... plas]

Are seats still available for...?
Est-ce qu'il reste des places pour...?
[es keel RestE de plas pooR...?]

What days is... showing?
Quels jours présente-t-on...?
[kel zhooR pRaysañt toñ...?]

Is it in the original version?
Est-ce en version originale?
[es añ veRsyoñ øReezheenal?]

Is it subtitled?
Est-ce sous-titré?
[es sooteetRay?]

Nightlife - *Vie nocturne*

---

bar	*bar*	[baR]
bartender	*barman*	[baRman]
cover charge ($)	*entrée ($)*	[añtRay]
dance	*danse*	[dañs]
dance floor	*piste de danse*	[peestE dE dañs]
discotheque	*discothèque*	[deeskøtek]
drink	*consommation*	[koñsømasyoñ]
gay bar	*bar gay*	[baR gay]
the gay scene	*le milieu gay*	[IE meelyœ gay]
jazz	*jazz*	[dzhaz]
lesbian bar	*bar lesbien*	[baR lesbyeñ]
live music	*musique en direct*	[mUzeek añ deeRekt]
musician	*musicien*	[mUzeesyeñ]
nightclub	*boîte de nuit*	[bwat dE nUee]
party	*partie*	[paRtee]
singer	*chanteur*	[shañtœR]
strip-tease	*strip-tease*	[stReepteez]
transvestite	*travesti*	[tRavestee]

ENTERTAINMENT

a drink/a glass	*un verre*	[œñ veR]
alcohol	*alcool*	[alkøl]
aperitif	*apéritif*	[apayReeteef]
beer	*bière*	[byeR]
Coke	*coca*	[koka]
coffee chaser	*digestif*	[deezhesteef]
flat mineral water	*eau minérale plate*	[o meenayRal plat]
imported drink	*boisson importée*	[bwasoñ eñpøRtay]
local drink	*boisson nationale*	[bwasoñ nasyønal]
mineral water	*eau minérale*	[o meenayRal]
sparkling mineral water	*eau minérale gazeuse*	[o meenayRal gazœz]
orange juice	*jus d'orange*	[zhU døRañzh]
soda water	*soda*	[soda]
tequila	*tequila*	[taykeela]
vermouth	*vermouth*	[veRmoot]
wine	*vin*	[veñ]

Meeting People - *Rencontres*

alone	*seul(e)*	[sœl]
beautiful	*beau / belle*	[bo / bel]
boy	*garçon*	[gaRsoñ]
charming	*charmant(e)*	[shaRmañ]

cheers (to toast)	*santé*	[sañtay]
compliment	*compliment*	[koñpleemañ]
conquest	*conquête*	[koñket]
couple	*couple*	[kooplE]
cute	*mignon(ne)*	[meengoñ(om)]
date	*rendez-vous*	[rañday voo]
discreet	*discret*	[deeskRe]
divorced	*divorcé(e)*	[deevøRsay]
drunk	*ivre*	[eevRE]
to flirt	*draguer*	[dRagay]
faithful	*fidèle*	[feedel]
girl / daughter	*fille*	[fee-y]
gay	*gay*	[gay]
to have a drink	*prendre un verre*	[pRañdRE œñ veR]
invitation	*invitation*	[eñveetasyoñ]
to invite	*inviter*	[eñveetay]
jealous	*jaloux(se)*	[zhaloo(z)]
macho	*macho*	[matsho]
man	*homme*	[øm]
married	*marié(e)*	[maRyay]
meeting	*rendez-vous*	[rañday voo]
nice	*sympathique*	[señpateek]
old	*vieux / vieille*	[vyœ / vye-y]
personality	*personnalité*	[peRsønaleetay]
pleased to meet you	*enchanté(e)*	[añshañtay]

play pool	*jouer au billard*	[zhway o beeyaR]
pretty	*joli(e)*	[zhølee]
safe sex	*sexe sûr*	[seksE sUR]
separated	*séparé(e)*	[saypaRay]
sexy	*sexy*	[seksee]
single	*célibataire*	[sayleebateR]
small	*petit(e)*	[pEtee(t)]
tall	*grand(e)*	[gRañ(d)]
tired	*fatigué(e)*	[fateegay]
ugly	*laid(e)*	[le(d)]
woman	*femme*	[fam]
young	*jeune*	[zhœn]

How are you?
Comment allez-vous?
[kømañ talay voo?]

Fine, and you?
Très bien, et vous?
[tRe byeñ, ay voo?]

I would like to introduce you to...
Je vous présente...
[zhE voo pRayzañt...]

Could you introduce me to this young lady?
Pourriez-vous me présenter à cette demoiselle?
[pooRyay voo mE pRayzañtay a set dEmwazel?]

What time do most people get here?
À quelle heure la plupart des gens viennent-ils?
[a kel œR la plUpaR de zhañ vyen teel?]

What time is the show?
À quelle heure est le spectacle?
[a kel œR e lE spektaklE?]

Hello, my name is...
Bonsoir, je m'appelle...
[boñswaR, zhE mapel...]

Do you like this music?
Est-ce que cette musique te plaît?
[es kE set mUseek tE ple?]

I am straight
Je suis hétéro (straight)
[zhE sUee zaytayRo]

I am gay
Je suis gay
[zhE sUee gay]

135

I am a lesbian
Je suis lesbienne
[zhE sUee lesbyen]

I am bisexual
Je suis bi-sexuel(le)
[zhE sUee beesexUel]

Is that your friend over there?
Est-ce que c'est ton ami, là-bas?
[es kE se toñ amee, laba?]

Which one,...
Lequel,...
[lEkel,...]

the blonde?	*le blond?*	[IE bloñ?]
the brunette?	*le châtain?*	[IE shateñ?]
the redhead?	*le roux?*	[IE Roo?]

Would you like a drink?
Est-ce que tu prends un verre?
[es kE tU pRañ œñ veR?]

What are you having?
Qu'est-ce que tu prends?
[kes kE tU pRañ?]

What country do you come from?
De quel pays viens-tu?
[dE kel pay-ee vyeñ tu?]

Are you here on vacation or for work?
Es-tu ici en vacances ou pour le travail?
[e tU eesee añ vakañs oo pooR lE tRava-y?]

What do you do in life? (see p 146)
Que fais-tu dans la vie?
[ke fe tU dañ la vee?]

Are you a student?
Es-tu étudiant(e)?
[e tU zaytUdyañ(t)?]

What are you studying?
Qu'étudies-tu?
[kaytUdee tU?]

Have you been living here long?
Habites-tu ici depuis longtemps?
[abeet tU eesee dEpUee loñtañ?]

Does your family live here too?
Ta famille vit-elle également ici?
[ta famee-y vee tel aygalmañ eesee?]

Do you have brothers and sisters? (see p 158)
As-tu des frères et sœurs?
[a tU de fReR ay sœR?]

Do you want to dance?
Est-ce que tu viens danser?
[es kE tU vyeñ dañsay?]

Let's find a quiet spot to talk
Cherchons un endroit tranquille pour bavarder
[sheRshoñ œñ añdRwa tRañkeel pooR bavaRday]

You are very cute
Tu es bien mignon(ne)
[tU e byeñ meengoñ(on)]

Do you have a boyfriend / girlfriend?
As-tu un ami (une amie)?
[a tU œñ namee (Un amee)?]

Too bad!
Quel dommage!
[kel dømazh!]

Do you like men/women?
Aimes-tu les garçons (les filles)?
[em tU le gaRsoñ (le fee-y)?]

138

Do you have children?
As-tu des enfants?
[a tU de zañfañ?]

Could we meet again tomorrow night?
Pouvons-nous nous revoir demain soir?
[poovoñ noo noo REvwaR dEmeñ swaR?]

When can I see you again?
Quand pouvons-nous nous revoir?
[kañ poovoñ noo noo REvwaR?]

I would like to invite you to dinner tomorrow night
J'aimerais t'inviter à dîner demain soir
[zhemRe teñveetay a deenay dEmeñ swaR]

Would you like to come to my place?
Tu viens chez moi?
[tU vyeñ shay mwa?]

Could we go to your place?
Pouvons-nous aller chez toi?
[poovoñ noo alay shay twa?]

I had an excellent evening with you
J'ai passé une excellente soirée avec toi
[zhay pasay Un ekselañt swaRay avek twa]

139

What time do the stores open?
À quelle heure ouvrent les boutiques?
[a kel œR oovRE le booteek?]

What time do the stores close?
À quelle heure ferment les boutiques?
[a kel œR feRmE le booteek?]

Are the stores open today?
Est-ce que les boutiques sont ouvertes aujourd'hui?
[es kE le booteek soñ tooveRt ozhooRdUee?]

What time do you close?
À quelle heure fermez-vous?
[a kel œR feRmay voo?]

What time do you open tomorrow?
À quelle heure ouvrez-vous demain?
[a kel œR oovRay voo dEmeñ?]

Do you have other stores?
Avez-vous d'autres succursales?
[avay voo dotRE sUkURsal?]

What is the price?

Quel est le prix?

[kel e lE pRee?]

How much does this cost?

Combien cela coûte-t-il?

[koñbyeñ sla koot teel?]

Do you have any less expensive ones?

En avez-vous des moins chers?

[añ avay voo de mweñ sheR?]

Could you give me a discount?

Pouvez-vous me faire un meilleur prix?

[poovay voo mE feR œñ me-yœR pRee?]

Do you take credit cards?

Est-ce que vous acceptez les cartes de crédit?

[es kE voo zakseptay le kaRt dE kRaydee?]

Where is the closest supermarket?

Où se trouve le supermarché le plus près d'ici?

[oo sE tRoov lE sUpeRmaRshay lE plU pRe deesee?]

shopping mall	*centre commercial*	[sañtRE kømeRsyal]
market	*marché*	[maRshay]

141

store / boutique	*boutique*	[booteek]
gift	*cadeau*	[kado]
postcard	*carte postale*	[kaRt pøstal]
stamps	*timbres*	[teñbRE]
clothing	*vêtements*	[vetmañ]

Specialties - *Spécialités*

I am looking for a... store.
Je cherche une boutique de...?
[zhE sheRsh Un booteek dE...]

| travel agent | *agent de voyages* | [azhañ dE vwa-yazh] |

I would like to change my return date
Je voudrais modifier ma date de retour
[zhE voodRe mødeefyay ma dat dE REtooR]

I would like to buy a ticket for...
Je voudrais acheter un billet pour...
[zhE voodRe ashtay œñ bee-ye pooR...]

| health foods | *aliments naturels* | [aleemañ natURel] |
| electronic equipment | *appareils électroniques* | [apaRe-y aylektRøneek] |

I would like a new battery for...

Je voudrais une nouvelle pile pour...

[zhE voodRe Un noovel peel pooR...]

barber	*coiffeur*	[kwafœR]
butcher	*boucherie*	[booshRee]
dry cleaner	*nettoyeur à sec*	[netwayER a sek]

Could you wash and iron this shirt for tomorrow?

Pouvez-vous laver et repasser cette chemise pour demain?

[poovay voo lavay ay REpasay set shEmeez pooR dEmeñ?]

hairdresser	*coiffeur*	[kwafœR]
handicrafts	*artisanat*	[aRteezana]
laudromat	*buanderie (libre-service)*	[bUañdRee (leebRE seRvees)]
shoes	*chaussures*	[shosUR]
music store	*disquaire*	[deeskeR]

Do you have a C.D. by...?

Avez-vous un disque de...?

[avay voo œñ deeskE dE...?]

What is the latest C.D. by...?

Quel est le plus récent disque de...?

[kel e lE plU Raysañ deeskE dE...?]

143

Could you play it for me?
Est-ce que vous pouvez me le faire entendre?
[es kE voo poovay mE lE feR añtañdRE?]

Could you tell me who sings...?
Pouvez-vous me dire qui chante...?
[poovay voo mE deeR kee shañt...?]

Do you have another C.D. by...?
Avez-vous un autre disque de...?
[avay voo œñ otRE deeskE dE...?]

photography equipment	*équipement photographique*	[aykeepmañ fotogRafeek]
computer equipment	*équipement informatique*	[aykeepmañ eñføRmateek]

Do you do repairs?
Faites-vous les réparations?
[fet voo le RaypaRasyoñ?]

How / Where can I log on to the Internet?
Comment / Où puis-je me brancher à Internet?
[kømañ / oo pUeezh mE bRañshay a eñteRnet?]

sports equipment (see p 90)	*équipement sportif*	[aykeepmañ spøRteef]

144

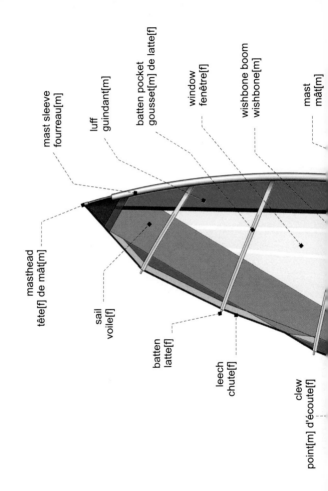

mast sleeve
fourreau[m]

luff
guindant[m]

batten pocket
gousset[m] de latte[f]

window
fenêtre[f]

wishbone boom
wishbone[m]

mast
mât[m]

masthead
tête[f] de mât[m]

sail
voile[f]

batten
latte[f]

leech
chute[f]

clew
point[m] d'écoute[f]

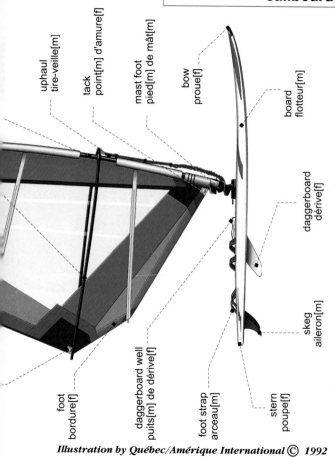

planche[f] à voile[f]
sailboard

uphaul
tire-veille[m]

tack
point[m] d'amure[f]

mast foot
pied[m] de mât[m]

bow
proue[f]

board
flotteur[m]

daggerboard
dérive[f]

skeg
aileron[m]

foot
bordure[f]

daggerboard well
puits[m] de dérive[f]

foot strap
arceau[m]

stern
poupe[f]

Illustration by Québec/Amérique International © 1992

fruits (see p 126) and vegetables (see p 113)	*fruits et légumes*	[fRUee zay laygUm]
toys	*jouets*	[zhwe]
bookstore	*librairie*	[leebReRee]
book	*livre*	[leevR]
coffee table book	*beau livre*	[bo leevR]
dictionary	*dictionnaire*	[deeksyoneR]
guide	*guide*	[geed]
literature	*littérature*	[leetayRatUR]
magazines	*magazines*	[magazeen]
map	*carte*	[kaRt]
more detailed map	*carte plus précise*	[kaRtE plU pRayseez]
newpapers	*journaux*	[zhooRno]
poetry	*poésie*	[po-ayzee]
road atlas	*atlas routier*	[atlas Rootyay]
street atlas	*répertoire des rues*	[RaypeRtwaR de RU]

Do you have books in English?
Avez-vous des livres en anglais?
[avay voo de leevR añ añgle?]

handicraft market	*marché d'artisanat*	[maRshay daRteezana]
public market	*marché public*	[maRshay pUbleek]

145

| supermarket | *marché* *d'alimentation* | [maRshay daleemañtasyoñ] |
| eye doctor | *oculiste* | [økUleest] |

I have broken my glasses
J'ai brisé mes lunettes
[zhay bReezay me lUnet]

I would like to replace my glasses
Je voudrais faire remplacer mes lunettes
[zhE voodRe feR Rañplasay me lUnet]

I have lost my glasses
J'ai perdu mes lunettes
[zhay peRdU me lUnet]

I have lost my contact lenses
J'ai perdu mes lentilles cornéennes
[zhay peRdU me lañtee-y køRnay-en]

Here is my prescription
Voici mon ordonnance
[vwasee moñ øRdønañs]

I should have a new eye exam
Je dois passer un nouvel examen de la vue
[zhE dwa pasay œñ noovel exameñ dE la vU]

beauty products	*produits de beauté*	[pRødUee dE botay]
fish store	*poissonnerie*	[pwasønRee]
hardware	*quincaillerie*	[keñka-y-Ree]
pharmacy / drugstore (see p 65)	*pharmacie*	[faRmasee]
supermarket	*supermarché*	[sUpeRmaRshay]
wines and spirits	*vins et liqueurs*	[veñ zay leekœR]

Clothing - *Vêtements*

children's clothing	*vêtements pour enfants*	[vetmañ pooR añfañ]
women's clothing	*vêtements pour dames*	[vetmañ pooR dam]
men's clothing	*vêtements pour hommes*	[vetmañ pooR øm]
sportswear	*vêtements sport*	[vetmañ spøR]
anorak	*anorak*	[anøRak]
bathing suit	*maillot de bain*	[ma-yo dE beñ]
bathrobe	*peignoir*	[pengwaR]
belt	*ceinture*	[señtUR]
boots	*bottes*	[bøt]
boxer shorts	*caleçon*	[kalsoñ]
bra	*soutien-gorge*	[sootyeñ gøRzh]
cap	*casquette*	[kasket]

147

coat	*manteau*	[mañto]
dress	*robe*	[Røb]
hat	*chapeau*	[shapo]
jacket	*veston*	[vestoñ]
jeans	*jean*	[dzheen]
men's suit jacket	*veste*	[vest]
pants	*pantalon*	[pañtaloñ]
pullover	*pull*	[pUl]
shirt	*jupe*	[zhUp]
shoes	*souliers*	[soolyay]
shorts	*short*	[shøRt]
skirt	*chemise*	[shEmeez]
socks	*bas (chaussettes)*	[ba (shoset)]
suit	*complet*	[koñple]
sweater	*chandail*	[shañda-y]
t-shirt	*t-shirt*	[teeshœRt]
tie	*cravate*	[kRavat]
underpants	*culotte*	[kUløt]
underwear	*sous-vêtement*	[soovetmañ]
windbreaker	*coupe-vent*	[koop vañ]
women's suit jacket	*tailleur*	[ta-yœR]

Could I try it on?

Est-ce que je peux l'essayer?

[es kE zhE pœ lese-yay?]

148

Do you have any... ones?
En avez-vous des plus...?
[añ avay voo de plU...?]

bigger	*grands*	[gRañd]
darker	*foncés*	[foñsay]
lighter	*clairs / légers*	[kleR] / [layzhay]
more economical	*économiques*	[aykønømeek]
roomier	*amples*	[añplE]
simpler	*simples*	[señplE]
smaller	*petits*	[pEtee]
softer	*souples*	[sooplE]
tighter	*serrés*	[seRay]
wider	*larges*	[laRzh]

Is it one hundred percent (100%) cotton?
Est-ce que c'est 100% coton?
[es kE se sañ pooR sañ køtoñ?]

What material is it made of?
C'est fait de quelle matière?
[se fe dE kel matyeR?]

Fabrics - *Tissus*

acrylic	*acrylique*	[akReeleek]
cotton	*coton*	[køtoñ]

149

linen	*lin*	[leñ]
polyester	*polyester*	[pølee-esteR]
rayon	*rayonne*	[Re-yøn]
silk	*soie*	[swa]
wool	*laine*	[len]

Could I try on a larger size?
Est-ce que je peux essayer une taille plus grande?
[es kE zhE pœ ese-yay Un ta-y plU gRañd?]

Could I try on a smaller size?
Est-ce que je peux essayer une taille plus petite?
[es kE zhE pœ ese-yay Un ta-y plU pEteet?]

Do you sew hems? do alterations?
Est-ce que vous faites les rebords? la retouche?
[es kE voo fet le REbøR? la REtoosh?]

Do I have to pay for alterations?
Est-ce qu'il faut payer pour la retouche ?
[es keel fo pe-yay pooR la REtoosh?]

When will it be ready?
Quand est-ce que ce sera prêt?
[kañ tes kE sE sERa pRe?]

Professions - *Les professions*

accountant	*comptable*	[koñtablE]
administator	*administrateur (trice)*	[admeenees-tRatœR(tRees)]
architect	*architecte*	[aRsheetekt]
artist	*artiste*	[aRteest]
athlete	*athlète*	[atlet]
banker	*banquier*	[bañkyay]
biologist	*biologiste*	[bee-oløzheest]
bookseller	*libraire*	[leebReR]
chef	*cuisinier(ère)*	[kUeezeenyay (eR)]
civil servant	*fonctionnaire*	[foñksyøneR]
computer expert	*informaticien(ne)*	[eñføRma-teesyeñ(en)]
dentist	*dentiste*	[dañteest]
designer	*designer*	[dayza-y̱-nœR]
dietician	*diététicien(ne)*	[dee-aytayteesyeñ(en)]
director	*directeur (trice)*	[deeRektœR (tRees)]
doctor	*médecin*	[maydseñ]

151

editor	*éditeur*	[aydeetœR]
engineer	*ingénieur(e)*	[eñzhaynyœR]
flight attendant	*agent de bord*	[azhañ dE bøR]
graphic artist	*graphiste*	[gRafeest]
hairdresser	*coiffeur(se)*	[kwafœR(fœz)]
journalist	*journaliste*	[zhooRnaleest]
lawyer	*avocat(e)*	[avoka(t)]
mechanic	*mécanicien(ne)*	[mayka-neesyeñ(en)]
military serviceman	*militaire*	[meeleeteR]
musician	*musicien(ne)*	[mUzeesyeñ(en)]
nurse	*infirmier(ère)*	[eñfeeRmyay(eR]
photographer	*photographe*	[fotogRaf]
pilot	*pilote*	[peeløt]
professor/teacher	*professeur(e)*	[pRøfesœR]
psychologist	*psychologue*	[pseekøløg]
publisher	*éditeur*	[aydeetœR]
retired	*retraité(e)*	[REtRetay]
salesperson	*vendeur(euse)*	[vañdœR(dœz)]
secretary	*secrétaire*	[sEkRayteR]
student	*étudiant(e)*	[aytUdyañ(t)]
technician	*technicien(ne)*	[tekneesyeñ(en)]
travel agent	*agent de voyages*	[azhañ dE vwayazh]
tour guide	*guide accompagnateur(trice)*	[geed akoñpanga-tœR(tRees)]
unemployed	*chômeur*	[shomœR]

urban planner	*urbaniste*	[URbaneest]
waiter	*serveur(euse)*	[seRvœR(vœz)]
worker	*ouvrier(ère)*	[oovRee-ay(eR)]
writer	*écrivain*	[aykReeveñ(en)]

In the Field of...
Dans le domaine...

---

construction	*de la construction*	[dE la koñstRUksyoñ]
design	*du design*	[dU dayza-y-n]
education	*de l'éducation*	[dE laydUkasyoñ]
electricity	*de l'électricité*	[de laylektReeseetay]
food service	*de la restauration*	[dE la RestoRasyoñ]
health	*de la santé*	[dE la sañtay]
investments	*des investissements*	[de zeñvesteesmañ]
publishing	*de l'édition*	[dE laydeesyoñ]
manufacturing	*manufacturier*	[manUfaktURyay]
media	*des médias*	[de maydya]
music	*de la musique*	[dE la mUzeek]
public sector	*public*	[pUbleek]
show business	*du spectacle*	[dU spektakl]
sport	*du sport*	[dU spøR]

telecommunications	*des télécommunications*	[de taylay-kømUneekasyoñ]
travel	*du voyage*	[dU vwayazh]

I am Studying...
J'étudie en...

accounting	*comptabilité*	[koñtabeeleetay]
administration	*administration*	[admeeneestRasyoñ]
architecture	*architecture*	[aRsheetektUR]
art	*art*	[aR]
biology	*biologie*	[bee-oløzhee]
computer science	*informatique*	[eñføRmateek]
economics	*économie*	[aykønømee]
engineering	*ingénierie*	[eñzhayneeRee]
environmental studies	*environnement*	[añveeRønmañ]
geography	*géographie*	[zhay-ogRafee]
graphic arts	*graphisme*	[gRafeesm]
history	*histoire*	[eestwaR]
journalism	*journalisme*	[zhooRnaleesm]
languages	*langues*	[lañg]
law	*droit*	[dRwa]
literature	*littérature*	[leetayRatUR]
medecine	*médecine*	[maydseen]
nursing	*nursing*	[nœRsing]

nutrition	*diététique*	[dee-aytayteek]
political science	*sciences politiques*	[syañs pøleeteek]
psychology	*psychologie*	[pseekøløzhee]
tourism	*tourisme*	[tooReesm]
urban planning	*urbanisme*	[URbaneesm]

I would like to introduce you to...
Je vous présente...
[zhE voo pRaysañt...]

Pleased to meet you
Enchanté
[añshañtay]

I would like to meet with... the director
J'aimerais avoir un rendez-vous avec... le directeur
[zhemRe avwaR œñ rañday voo avek... lE deeRektœR]

   ...the person in charge
   ...la personne responsable
   [...la peRsøn Respoñsablε]

Could I have the name of the person in charge...?
Puis-je avoir le nom de la personne responsable...?
[pUeezh avwaR le noñ dE la peRsøn Respoñsablε...?]

of marketing	*du marketing*	[dU maRkEting]
of accounting	*de la comptabilité*	[dE la koñtabeeleetay]
of imports	*des importations*	[de zeñpøRtasyoñ]
of exports	*des exportations*	[de zekspøRtasyoñ]
of sales	*des ventes*	[de vañt]
of purchasing	*des achats*	[de zasha]
of human resources	*du personnel*	[dU peRsønel]

It is urgent
C'est urgent
[se tURzhañ]

I am..., from the company...
Je suis..., de la société...
[zhE sUee..., dE la søsyaytay...]

She is not here at the moment
Elle n'est pas ici en ce moment
[el ne pa zeesee añ smømañ]

She has gone out
Elle est sortie
[el e søRtee]

When will she be back?
Quand sera-t-elle de retour?
[kañ sERa tel dE REtooR?]

Could you ask her/him to call me?
Pouvez-vous lui demander de me rappeler?
[poovay voo lUee dEmañday dE mE Raplay]

I am stopping over in Paris for three days
Je suis de passage à Paris pour trois jours
[zhE sUee dE pasazh a paree pooR tRwa zhooR]

I am at the hotel... You can reach me at..., room...
*Je suis à l'hôtel... Vous pouvez me joindre au...,
chambre...*
[zhE sUee a lotel... voo poovay mE zhweñdR o...,
shañbRE...]

I would like to meet with you briefly
J'aimerais vous rencontrer brièvement
[zhemRe voo RañkoñtRay bRee-evmañ]

to show you our new product
pour vous présenter notre nouveau produit
[pooR voo pRayzañtay nøtRE noovo pRødUee]

to discuss a project
pour discuter d'un projet
[pooR deeskUtay dœñ pRøzhe]

We are looking for a distributor for...
Nous cherchons un distributeur pour...
[noo sheRshoñ œñ deestReebUtER pooR...]

We would like to import your product, the...
Nous aimerions importer votre produit, le...
[noo zemERyoñ eñpøRtay vøtRE pRødUee, lE...]

FAMILY - *FAMILLE*

brother	*frère*	[fReR]
sister	*sœur*	[sœR]
my brothers and sisters	*mes frères et sœurs*	[me fReR ay sœR]
mother	*mère*	[meR]
father	*père*	[peR]
son	*fils*	[fees]
daughter	*fille*	[fee-y]
grandmother	*grand-mère*	[gRañ meR]
grandfather	*grand-père*	[gRañ peR]
nephew	*neveu*	[nEvœ]
niece	*nièce*	[nyes]

cousin	*cousin(e)*	[koozeñ]
brother-in-law	*beau-frère*	[bo fReR]
sister-in-law	*belle-sœur*	[bel sœR]

SENSATIONS AND EMOTIONS
SENSATIONS ET ÉMOTIONS

I am hungry
J'ai faim
[zhay feñ]

We are hungry
Nous avons faim
[noo zavoñ feñ]

He is hungry
Il a faim
[eel a feñ]

She is hungry
Elle a faim
[el a feñ]

I am thirsty
J'ai soif
[zhay swaf]

I am tired
Je suis fatigué(e)
[zhE sUee fateegay]

I am cold
J'ai froid
[zhay fRwa]

I am hot
J'ai chaud
[zhay sho]

I am sick
Je suis malade
[zhE sUee malad]

I am happy
Je suis content(e)
[zhE sUee koñtañ(t)]

I am happy
Je suis heureux / heureuse
[zhE sUee zœRœ(z)]

I am satisfied
Je suis satisfait(e)
[zhE sUee sateesfe(t)]

I am sorry
Je suis désolé(e)
[zhE sUee dayzølay]

I am disappointed
Je suis déçu(e)
[zhE sUee daysU]

I am bored
Je m'ennuie
[zhE mañ-nUee]

I have had enough
J'en ai assez
[zhañ ay asay]

I cannot wait to...
Je suis impatient(e) de...
[zhE sUee zeñpasyañ(t) dE...]

I am getting impatient
Je m'impatiente
[zhE meñpasyañt]

I am lost
Je suis égaré(e)
[zhE sUee zaygaRay]

Christmas Day	*le jour de Noël*	[lE zhooR dE nøel]
New Year's Day	*le jour de l'An*	[lE zhooR dE lañ]
Epiphany	*le jour des Rois*	[lE zhooR de Rwa]
Mardi Gras / Shrove Tuesday	*le Mardi gras*	[lE maRdee gRa]
Ash Wednesday	*le mercredi des Cendres*	[lE meRkREdee de sañdRE]
Good Friday	*le Vendredi saint*	[lE vañdREdee señ]
Holy Week	*la Semaine sainte*	[la sEmen señt]
Easter Sunday	*le jour de Pâques*	[lE zhooR dE pak]
Easter Monday	*le lundi de Pâques*	[lE lœñdee dE pak]
May Day	*la fête des Travailleurs*	[la fet de tRava-yœR]
Mother's Day	*la fête des Mères*	[la fet de meR]
Father's Day	*la fête des Pères*	[la fet de peR]
National Holiday	*la Fête nationale*	[la fet nasyønal]
Labour Day	*la fête du Travail*	[la fet Du tRava-y]
Thanksgiving	*l'Action de grâce*	[laksyoñ dE gRas]
Veteran's Day	*l'Armistice*	[laRmeestees]
Remembrance Day	*le jour du Souvenir*	[lE zhooR dU soovneeR]
Boxing Day	*le lendemain de Noël*	[lE lañdmeñ dE nøel]

St. Patrick's Day	*la Saint-Patrick*	[la señ patReek]
Victoria Day	*la fête de la Reine*	[la fet dE la Ren]
Memorial Day	Memorial Day	[*Memorial Day*]
Presidents Day	*le jour des Présidents*	[lE zhooR de pRayzeedañ]
Independence Day	*le jour de l'Indépendance*	[lE zhooR dE leñdaypañdañs]

INDEX OF ENGLISH WORDS

The letter P, followed by the letters A, B, C, D, E, and F, refers to the corresponding colour plate.

INDEX OF
FRENCH WORDS

181

INDEX OF FRENCH WORDS

INDEX OF
FRENCH WORDS

Order Form

Ulysses Travel Guides

☐ Acapulco	$14.95 CAN $9.95 US		☐ Islands of the Bahamas	$24.95 CAN $17.95 US
☐ Atlantic Canada	$24.95 CAN $17.95 US		☐ Las Vegas	$17.95 CAN $12.95 US
☐ Bahamas	$24.95 CAN $17.95 US		☐ Lisbon	$18.95 CAN $13.95 US
☐ Beaches of Maine	$12.95 CAN $9.95 US		☐ Louisiana	$29.95 CAN $21.95 US
☐ Bed & Breakfasts in Québec	$14.95 CAN $10.95 US		☐ Martinique	$24.95 CAN $17.95 US
☐ Belize	$16.95 CAN $12.95 US		☐ Montréal	$19.95 CAN $14.95 US
☐ Calgary	$17.95 CAN $12.95 US		☐ Miami	$9.95 CAN $12.95 US
☐ Canada	$29.95 CAN $21.95 US		☐ New Orleans	$17.95 CAN $12.95 US
☐ Chicago	$19.95 CAN $14.95 US		☐ New York City	$19.95 CAN $14.95 US
☐ Chile	$27.95 CAN $17.95 US		☐ Nicaragua	$24.95 CAN $16.95 US
☐ Colombia	$29.95 CAN $21.95 US		☐ Ontario	$27.95 CAN $19.95US
☐ Costa Rica	$27.95 CAN $19.95 US		☐ Ontario's Best Hotels and Restaurants	$27.95 CAN $19.95US
☐ Cuba	$24.95 CAN $17.95 US		☐ Ottawa	$17.95 CAN $12.95 US
☐ Dominican Republic	$24.95 CAN $17.95 US		☐ Panamá	$24.95 CAN $17.95 US
☐ Ecuador and Galápagos Islands	$24.95 CAN $17.95 US		☐ Peru	$27.95 CAN $19.95 US
☐ El Salvador	$22.95 CAN $14.95 US		☐ Phoenix	$16.95 CAN $12.95 US
☐ Guadeloupe	$24.95 CAN $17.95 US		☐ Portugal	$24.95 CAN $16.95 US
☐ Guatemala	$24.95 CAN $17.95 US		☐ Provence - Côte d'Azur	$29.95 CAN $21.95US
☐ Hawaii	$29.95 CAN $21.95 US		☐ Puerto Rico	$24.95 CAN $17.95 US
☐ Honduras	$24.95 CAN $17.95 US			